BUILDING BELOW THE WATERLINE

GORDON MacDONALD

BUILDING BELOW THE WATERLINE

Shoring Up the Foundations of Leadership

HENDRICKSON PUBLISHERS

Building Below the Waterline

Hendrickson Publishers Marketing, LLC
P. O. Box 3473
Peabody, Massachusetts 01961-3473

© 2011 by Gordon MacDonald

ISBN 978-1-59856-669-7

Except where otherwise noted, Scripture taken from THE HOLY BIBLE, NEW INTERNATIONAL VERSION®, NIV® Copyright © 1973, 1978, 1984, 2010 by Biblica, Inc.™ Used by permission. All rights reserved worldwide.

Printed in the United States of America

First Printing — April 2011

TABLE OF CONTENTS

123698

PART TWO: THE OUTER LIFE OF A LEADER

INTRODUCTION

David McCullough's book *The Great Bridge* tells a fascinating story about the building of the Brooklyn Bridge, which arches the East River and joins Manhattan to Brooklyn.

In June 1872, the chief engineer of the project wrote: "To such of the general public as might imagine that no work had been done on the New York tower, because they see no evidence of it above the water, I should simply remark that the amount of the masonry and concrete laid on that foundation during the past winter, *under water,* is equal in quantity to the entire masonry of the Brooklyn tower visible today above the waterline" (italics mine).

The Brooklyn Bridge remains a major transportation artery in New York City today because 135 years ago the chief engineer and his construction team did their most patient and daring work where no one could see it: on the foundations of the towers below the waterline. It is one more illustration of an ageless principle in leadership: the work done below the waterline (in a leader's soul) that determines whether he or she will stand the test of time and challenge. This work is called worship, devotion, spiritual discipline. It's done in quiet, where no one but God sees.

Today, there is a tremendous emphasis on leadership themes such as vision, organizational strategy, and the "market-sensitivity" of one's message. It's all great stuff—stuff I wish I'd heard when I was a young pastor. But if it is all about what's above the waterline, we are likely to witness a leadership crash of sorts in the coming years. Leaders blessed with great natural skills and charisma may be vulnerable to collapse in their character, their key relationships, and their center of belief because they never learned that one cannot (or should not) build *above* the waterline until there is a substantial foundation *below* it.

Gordon MacDonald

PART ONE

THE INNER LIFE

OF A LEADER

FINDING YOUR CENTER

*The soul's center is God. When it has reached God
with all the capacity of its being and the strength
of its operation and inclination, it will have
attained to its final and deepest center in God.*

ST. JOHN OF THE CROSS

There was a time when I would have been jealous for leadership; today, I find it sobering. I have passed the point of aspiring to leadership. It is a privilege to be a leader, but the price is great.

A leader has to watch every word he or she says and quickly learns that you can't go through life without a few critics, some well deserved. Occasionally, leaders have a rough time knowing who's a genuine friend, and there are serious time limitations on pursuing healthy relationships. There's pressure on friends and family, and at times most leaders, I suspect, ask, "Who needs all this?"

On the other hand, everything I've been privileged to be part of has been the result of a choice to respond to God's call to leadership. So I'm not whining about the pressure.

It comes back to God's anointing. My wife, Gail, and I are constantly aware that God has called us to do something. Every morning, we take time to ask God, "What is the purpose of this in our lives?" I no longer entertain the notion that whatever I'm supposed to do has to be great, but I do feel strongly a sense of call and obligation. Besides the Lord's anointing, what other traits must the Christian leader possess?

Four Traits of a Christian Leader

The first trait of a leader is the ability to communicate vision. The leader is the custodian of a vision. Some of us communicate the vision through our gift of speaking, but others have done it differently. D. E. Hoste, for example, Hudson Taylor's successor at China Inland Mission, was an administrator, and his leadership was accomplished in the office and at the committee table. His wisdom and ability to persuade convinced people that he was filled with the Holy Spirit and worthy to be followed.

The second trait of a Christian leader is sensitivity to people. First and foremost, a leader must hear what people are saying. Peter Drucker says communication doesn't happen with the speaker but with the hearers. As a speaker, I've got to understand the way you think. How do you perceive information? Churchill knew the English people, so he was sensitive to the right word forms that would capture their attention— he knew what would inspire them and make them mad enough at the enemy to keep persevering despite incredible hardship.

A third trait a leader must possess is the ability to assess situations. Being sensitive also means developing the ability to look at situations and decode what's going on. I think God has given me a gift in this area. It's instinctive for me to walk into a room and quickly sense who is in charge, or for that matter, to quickly realize that no one is in charge. That's an important skill in church situations.

The fourth trait is keen self-knowledge. Sensitive leaders need to know themselves. If we don't know ourselves and what shaped us, what neutralizes us, and what our limits are, we invite disaster. Many men and women in leadership positions are insecure. Some struggle with large unresolved areas from the past. Unless the past can be resolved, it often becomes an Achilles' heel in leadership.

Let me give an example. I came into the ministry as an insecure person, specifically needing affirmation. I needed for people to like me, and I equated applause with affirmation. I've had to transition from being a driven person to being a called person.

The resolution to know oneself begins through daily self-examination against God's righteousness and the discovery of sinful motives. Second, it's going back in your past to ask: *What has formed me? What am I looking for in life? What didn't I get that I needed?*

The Value of a Mentor

A valuable resource to help with this is a mentor. A mentor provides affirmation, so you don't have to look for it in artificial ways. Second, a mentor provides correction. In seminary I sat under the teaching of Ray Buker. For another course, I was to present a position paper in a Christian education debate, so I cut two classes I had with Dr. Buker that day to work on it. That night, after I read the paper and everyone had left, Buker came up and said, "Gordon, that was a good paper you read. Unfortunately, it wasn't a great one. Would you like to know *why* it wasn't a great one?"

I said, "I'm not sure, but . . ."

"It was not great because you sacrificed the routine to write it."

That was one of those open-window moments where I recognized a real life principle. Sacrificing the routine is not what makes one effective. Dr. Buker was trying to point out that most of us go through life for the peaks, rather than realizing that life is often lived in the valleys and on the hillsides. I never forgot that lesson.

When I was an athlete, I lost a very important race because I didn't listen to my coach. Afterward, he said to me, "You have all the promise of being a man who's going to go through life learning things the hard way."

I walked off the field that day thinking, *That's the last lesson I'm going to learn the hard way. I'm going to learn by other people's hard ways.* That principle has stuck with me. I began to observe others' failures and humiliation, and then I would ask myself, *Where would I be apt to make that same error?*

Many leaders operate at a level where they can go for a long time without anybody calling them to account, and as a result, they get so busy helping other people that their perceptions drift. A mentor comes along, asks the hard questions, makes the stiff confrontation, and the leader suddenly realizes, *How could I not have seen this?*

Your Spiritual Center

We isolate both the positive and that which we must discard. We could all use our backgrounds as an excuse to say, "This is why I am like this, so take me the way I am." But as leaders, we can't afford that kind of self-pity. This is hard work, and it's a lifelong process. I could go back to being a driven man pretty quickly if I didn't maintain a spiritual center.

I'm convinced from my reading of the mystics that our perception of reality revolves around a spiritual center. That center quickly becomes almost inoperative if it's not maintained through constant spiritual discipline. Almost all Christian leaders believe that doctrinally, but few believe it experientially enough to carve out one or two hours a day to maintain their spiritual center.

What results is an accumulation of knowledge without wisdom. You get leaders who operate on charisma instead of spiritual power. And it takes spiritual power to make the clear break with the world's values, as a spiritual leader must. I don't mean to sound pious, but as I get older I realize this truth more and more. We can't maintain the pace unless we pray, study Scripture, and read heavy doses of the classical spiritual literature.

On the other hand, when we lead from within, our own resources are channeled and multiplied from that very powerful spiritual center where transformation happens.

FOR FURTHER REFLECTION

1. How sensitive are you to other people and situations? What impact has this had on your development as a leader? What steps could you take to develop this type of sensitivity?

2. What mentors have you encountered in your life up to this point? Think back on coaches, spiritual directors, and other leaders who have shaped your thinking and habits. What were the key lessons they imparted?

3. How much time do you set aside for spiritual reflection and prayer? How could you adjust your schedule to increase this time?

SIX WORDS TO LIVE BY

Present to God . . . present to people.

CHARLES DE FOUCAULD

I am romanced by the simple phrase by which Charles de Foucauld (1858–1916) chose to define his life: "Present to God . . . present to people." In the morass of mission statements and pithy slogans designed to identify the passions of organizations, churches, and individuals, I think I like this one best.

Being present reminds me of the experience my wife and I once had while on a walk in a Swiss alpine valley. We had come upon a farmer and his dog who were rounding up a large herd of brown cows (the ones with the huge bells around their necks). The farmer would point to a spot out on the edge of the herd. The dog would race in that direction, then suddenly stop to look back to get a second command. The farmer would sweep his hand to the right or left, and the dog, now furiously barking, would drive the cows wherever the farmer was willing them to go.

Then the dog would tear back to the farmer's side, sit, breathing hard, and look up waiting—almost impatiently—for the farmer's next order. For some reason, that picture of a dog who is so present to his master—ready to respond—shows me what it must mean to fit Foucauld's definition of life.

Present to God

I can be present to God by making sure that I am quiet enough to hear some of the kinds of whispering that Elijah heard on the mountain. By being sensitive to the kinds of directives that Philip heard when he was directed to the chariot of the Ethiopian. By being awake enough to discern the same voice that spoke to Paul one night when he was told not to be afraid, to keep on speaking, not to be silent, "for I am with you . . . and I have many people in this city" (Acts 18:10). By being present to God's love, to God's rebukes, to God's revelations of himself.

Oswald Chambers writes, "Do not have as your motive the desire to be known as a praying [person]. Get an inner chamber in which to pray where no one knows you are praying, shut the door, and talk to God in secret. Have no other motive than to know your Father in heaven."

Present to People

Is this harder or easier than being present to God? I find it easy to be present—doesn't everyone?—to attractive people, advantaged people, visionary people, intelligent people, likeable people. I love being present to people who like me and find me witty and charming. My grandchildren fit this category.

But present to people who are weak, poor, sick, grumpy, unreliable, unthankful, and disrespectful? That's another story. My instinct is, all too often, to be absent to them. And it's here that my character and call get challenged every day. Sometimes I win; often I lose in this being present business. Because being present to people means that I must listen extra carefully, listen, and then respond. And that can be inconvenient and too taxing.

So I like Foucauld's phrase that reduces complex issues and busy schedules to six simple words. We call that an elevator story—something said in a matter of seconds that defines a whole life.

FOR FURTHER REFLECTION

1. *Do you have a personal mission statement? If not, create one. Can you condense it to just six words?*

2. *In addition to the ways listed, how are you present to God?*

3. *Do you find it easy or hard to be present to people? How can you become more actively present to those around you?*

CULTIVATING THE SOUL

Spirit of the living God, be the Gardener of my soul . . .
Clear away the dead growth of the past, break up
the hard clods of custom and routine, stir in the rich
compost of vision and challenge. Bury deep in my
soul the implanted Word, cultivate and tend my
heart, until new life buds and opens and flowers.

RICHARD FOSTER

Thirty years ago, Gail and I purchased an old farm and called it Peace Ledge. During the 1800s, the land's valuable timber had been clear-cut and transformed into pasture where enormous workhorses could be bred and raised. Then, around 1900, the farm went belly-up, was abandoned, and, after seventy years, became a forest again.

Occasionally, Gail and I select a small piece of this woodland and clear it. We eliminate unhealthy trees. We rip out the kind of ground vegetation that makes for fire danger. And we dig away the ubiquitous boulders (the gift of ancient glaciers) that might create havoc with the blades of our tractor mower.

Gail and I enjoy our accomplishments—for a little while—until our eyes begin to spot more work begging attention in adjoining areas we hadn't considered before. This refreshing of our land is a lifelong task. And when we die, our descendents, presumably, will continue the job.

For me, this outdoor labor mirrors the discipline of spiritual formation, for just as one cultivates the land, so one must regularly, systematically even, cultivate the deepest parts of the interior life where God is most likely to whisper (not shout) the everlasting promises into one's life.

Spiritual formation involves cutting, weeding, digging, raking, and planting—not with a chainsaw or shovel, of course, but through the work of worship, reflection, prayer, study, and a score of other soul-oriented activities described in books by Richard Foster, Dallas Willard, and Henri Nouwen, to name a few.

When a piece of our land is renewed, Gail and I are always surprised at the beauty that occurs almost overnight. Wildflowers bloom; forest animals visit; good trees mature. The virtues of creation just seem to appear. And when the soul is similarly attended to, there appear the virtues of godly character.

Frankly, I don't think a lot of men and women in leadership know this. I mean *really know* it. What drives my opinion are these impressions.

First, the primary subject matter of most training and motivational conferences on leadership: vision, clever, well-researched programs, and growing large, successful institutions. Admittedly good stuff. But missing is the recognition that soul cultivation goes before institution building. How do you grow large, healthy, and authentic churches (the current rage) without growing the soul of a leader, which sustains the effort over the long haul?

A second impression: the dreadful casualty list of men and women who do not make it to a tenth anniversary in Christian ministry. Burnout, failure, and disillusionment are exacting a terrible toll. I'm amazed how many leaders just disappear, just drop off the edge.

A third: the constant conversations I have with younger men and women. They confide that they are spiritually dry, unmotivated, despairing, and wondering what to do about it.

And maybe there's a fourth: I never forget how close—how really close—I myself came to missing the cut. Though my own defining moment of personal crisis came years ago, the memory is always fresh.

Forming the Soul's Core

St. Paul's words to Timothy are too easily ignored in this high-pitched, high-casualty leadership lifestyle of ours: "Train yourself to be godly . . . godliness has value for all things, holding promise for both the present life and the life to come" (1 Tim. 4:7–8). I smell spiritual formation in these remarks.

The forming of the soul that it might be a dwelling place for God is the primary work of the Christian leader. This is not an add-on, an option, or a third-level priority. Without this core activity, one almost guarantees that he or she will not last in leadership for a lifetime, or that what work is accomplished will become less and less reflective of God's honor and God's purposes.

In his twenties, William Booth, the founder of the Salvation Army, wrote a letter to his wife describing his feelings of discouragement and ineffectiveness. He was close to quitting, he said. Catherine, a remarkable woman, wrote back:

> I know how possible it is to preach and pray and sing, and even shout, while the heart is not right with God. I know how popularity and prosperity have a tendency to elate and exalt self, if the heart is not humble before God. I know how Satan takes advantage of these things

to work out the destruction (if possible) of one whom the Lord uses to pull down strongholds of his kingdom, and all these considerations make me tremble, and weep, and pray for you, my dearest love, that you may be able to overcome all his devices, and having done all to stand, not in your own strength but in humble dependence on him who worketh "all in all."

As far as I can tell, Catherine was twenty-three when she wrote these words. But she was not too young to "get it." William's spiritual core, she understood, was the key to everything.

I shall leave the techniques of spiritual formation to other, more qualified spiritual directors. What occupies my thoughts presently are the evidential virtues that spring—like wildflowers—out of a soul aligned with heaven.

Anthony Bloom writes of a desert father who was invited to preach at a Mass where a visiting bishop would be in attendance. The monastic refused, saying, "If my silence doesn't speak to him, my words will be useless."

The monk's point provokes me because I spend a large part of my life depending upon words, social skills, and an ability to think quickly on my feet to communicate with people. But how would I communicate if I were limited to silence? It could only happen if there were virtues growing out of my soul like flowers erupting from a renewed piece of ground.

Five Virtues to Cultivate

What virtues might those be? With caution, I nominate five that are all too often in short supply and which, if long neglected, will signal our demise. The list is neither exhaustive nor guaranteed to be the best. But it's mine.

Harvested Humility

First of all, I would wish that people would see that, as a result of my soul work, I have made progress in humility. Humility is not something one achieves; it is the result of other pursuits.

To be frank, people who knew me in the earlier years would never have associated me with humility. I fear such people would remember me as full of self, perhaps overconfident, endlessly in motion. Talented, a bit gifted perhaps, but not a humble man.

"A humble man," Isaak of Syria said, "is never hurried, hasty, or perturbed, but at all times remains calm. Nothing can ever surprise, disturb, or dismay him, for he suffers neither fear nor change in tribulations, neither surprise nor elation in enjoyment. All his joy and gladness are in what is pleasing to the Lord."

If even a sliver of the virtue of humility grows out of the ground of my soul today, it is only because I am old enough to be well acquainted with the overpowering effects of sin, the realities of personal limits and liabilities, and the corrosive effects of perpetual accomplishment. Beyond that it is because I have slowly (!) come to appreciate the grandeur of God and my place before him as a small child.

"The way of the Christian leader," wrote Henri Nouwen, "is not the way of upward mobility in which the world has invested so much, but the way of downward mobility ending on the cross. . . . It is not a leadership of power and control, but a leadership of powerlessness and humility in which the suffering servant of God, Jesus Christ, is made manifest."

Nouwen's words drip with mystery. They make little sense in a life where planning, promotion, creativity, and charisma seem to mean everything. But this is the direction for the leader who lasts and who, in the end, may not produce large institutions but will eventually produce great saints.

Productive Compassion

If I were forced into silence, I would wish, second, that people would see the evidence of compassion as a product of my soul work. Compassion: the ability to identify at heart level with the vulnerabilities, fears, and sorrows of others. And to identify in such a way that one is not paralyzed but energized with great love.

An email came to me from someone who wished to know whether or not they would really be welcomed in our congregation if certain secrets in their life were revealed. "I don't want to be somebody's project," this person wrote.

Those words bored into my soul because I realize how easy it is to slot people, as projects, into programs and bypass the taxing experience of authentic identification with struggle.

I'll be frank with my opinion. The larger world is not picking up the signals of compassion from the branch of Christianity of which I am a part. While Nicholas Kristof of the *New York Times* often applauds our movement for its far-flung programs in AIDS, home-building, hospitals, and disaster response, we are not known as compassionate people as we do these things. All our good efforts are covered by the sense that we are proud, angry, and vindictive in our selective approaches to those needing some form of redemption.

I don't want to be perceived as a hard person with an accusatory message who occasionally does good deeds. Much better to be perceived as the wounded healer who exchanges his bandages with the one who has none to offer back.

Steadfastness, Not Stubbornness

If I were to live in total silence, I would wish, thirdly, that spiritual formation would produce steadfastness in me. Steadfastness is not stubbornness, nor is it a resistance to change. Instead, it is a ceaseless embrace of certain purposes and commitments from which one will never retreat.

Steadfastness means reliability of character, fulfillment of promises, faithfulness to key relationships, and (most important) living in obedience to Jesus. Such steadfastness has not been a part of my nature. If it is part of me today, it is because I have had to acquire it. The impulse to quit, to avoid, to cut and run comes naturally to me, and were it not for some mentors and a very strong wife who challenged me to face this, I have no idea where I'd be today.

It was in the process of spiritual formation that I faced down the "quitter's gene" that lives in me. Through rebuke, through the inspiration of the lives of the biblical greats (and the saints beyond them), and through the encouragement of my personal community, I acquired something of the discipline of steadfastness. Today, I like to think that I'm a pretty good "sticker," but without the continual restoring of the soul, it just wouldn't have happened.

"Be ye stedfast, unmoveable, always abounding," Paul wrote to the Corinthians (1 Cor. 15:58 KJV). He was obviously driving at something important. Perhaps he was speaking to people who were habitually undependable, short-lived in their commitments, caving in to pressure—people like the natural me.

Faith Beyond Sight

If words were taken from me, I would hope that others would see faith in me. Faith: an ability to trust in and draw upon the power of God beyond my rationality, my instinctive pessimism, my willingness to settle for less than best.

I love to read about and observe faith-driven people, and this is part of my spiritual formation activities. Faithful people inspire me. I can't get enough of John Wesley, William Wilberforce, the Countess of

Huntingdon, and Charles Simeon: all eighteenth-century evangelicals who had the temerity to believe that the Gospel of Jesus Christ could alter the social fabric of England. When I finish with any of them in my books, I'm ready to spring into motion, believing God for such transformations today.

I'm often drawn to the Bible story of the poor widow who put her two "mites" in the temple treasury and gave, according to Jesus, "all she had" (Luke 21:2–4). That's faith in a nutshell: a calm, quiet, unostentatious offering of all her assets, believing that God would provide for her needs.

Spiritual formation means building a heart that is comfortable in asking for and believing in God to do the seemingly impossible. Praying for healing of the sick, the transformation of the wicked, the lifting of the hand of the oppressor.

There is an intimate connection between faith and vision. I see a lot of both when it comes to building institutions and buildings. I guess I would like to demonstrate my own faith and vision less in institutions and more in the possibilities that God has for people.

Self-Control

If my life, like the monk in Anthony Bloom's story, were to be lived in silence, I would hope that the spiritual fruit of self-control would be in evidence.

This, of course, has a lot to do with discipline and one's willingness to cultivate the ability to say no to wrong as well as yes to the right things in life. Not a popular subject, really.

Self-control is in play when a leader is opposed, slandered, unappreciated, ignored, or required to go the second mile. How does he or she respond? Self-control speaks to our use of money, our handling of power and influence, and our response to inflated adulation. How do we bring healthy limits to our lives?

The Old Testament offers several portraits of individuals who lacked self-control: Samson, Saul, and Solomon come to mind. And the champions? Joseph, of course. And Daniel. And Esther.

When I imagine self-control at its fullest, I picture Jesus in the garden of Gethsemane surrounded by failing friends, cruel soldiers who have come to arrest him, and the scurrilous Judas Iscariot. What a time to lose one's cool! But he didn't. He kept his dignity and became the calm center of a wildly chaotic situation. That's self-control.

"It is the quality of leaders that they can bear to be sat on, absorb shocks, act as a buffer, bear being much plagued," wrote Fred Mitchell, a one-time leader in the old China Inland Mission. "The wear and tear and the continual friction and trials which come to the servants of God are the greatest tests of character."

Ongoing Formation

Outside the window of the little study I maintain here at Peace Ledge is a large boulder. It would probably take a box four feet high, wide, and deep if I were going to ship it someplace. Many years ago the boulder was buried in the ground, and only an inch or two of it poked through the soil. My wife, thinking it to be a minor task, began to dig it up.

The more she dug, the more she realized how big a project she'd undertaken. But there was no going back now. Two days later, we (now she had me involved) were removing this gargantuan piece of stone from a hole big enough for a swimming pool (I exaggerate to make my point). As I write this piece, I can see the once-submerged boulder out my window.

The stone remains a constant reminder of spiritual formation. Some things need to be dug out. Still more things need to be cut away. Other things need to be planted. Then, in the long run, you have something beautiful. Really beautiful.

And you don't need words to tell other people what they're seeing. They observe God at work in your life—even if there is only silence. Spiritual formation can happen without saying a word.

FOR FURTHER REFLECTION

1. *Which of the five virtues mentioned are evident in your life? How have they been cultivated? Are any of the five virtues lacking in your life?*

2. *What authors feed you spiritually on a regular basis? How do they influence your own spiritual formation?*

3. *How can you balance the drive to succeed and the vision for growth with being the type of leader Henri Nouwen describes (see page 19)?*

WHAT I WANT TO BE WHEN I GROW UP

*I urge you to live a life worthy
of the calling you have received.*

EPHESIANS 4:1

For two of the years I was in seminary, I pastored a tiny country church 175 miles east of Denver. For a year, Gail and I saved money by living in the church's small parsonage. That meant that on Tuesday at 4 A.M. I would leave the house and make a three-hour drive to Denver in our Volkswagen Beetle.

The drive along Route 36 from the Kansas border to Denver was almost a straight shot. As I looked westward to the horizon, I sensed that the car could go in any direction and never run into a barrier. It was smooth sailing.

Life is sometimes like that. No barriers. You feel, *I can do anything I want if I am willing to work hard enough. And pray hard enough. And study hard enough.* I once believed that myself.

But back to Route 36. Just beyond the town of Last Chance, Colorado, suddenly there are three mountain peaks on the horizon—Pike's

Peak to the south, Long's Peak to the north, and Mount Evans directly to the west. Instantly the illusion of a barrierless journey is pricked by the realization that three solid and rather large obstacles represent a reduction in options.

Sometimes, in leadership, we also reach a "Last Chance." The day comes when you discover personal barriers and limits: *I cannot do this as well as . . . I don't actually have the gift of . . . This task requires something that simply isn't my strength.*

Obligations are accrued. Perhaps a spouse. Maybe a child or two. Perhaps responsibilities to extended family members. They wouldn't be complimented by being called barriers. But they nevertheless cut down on other options.

This can be a tough moment for young leaders. The once dizzying dreams are slowly modified by reality. And little by little, we discover why we're really in this "business" of serving God. We're probably not going to be heroes, and the world is not going to beat a path to our door begging for our insights. And that's okay.

But let me finish my parable.

On the trip to Denver, as you near the city, there comes a point where the long stretch of the Rocky Mountains rises up like an impenetrable wall. Where once only three barriers, evenly spaced apart, interrupted the horizon, now multiple barriers fill your vision. You get the feeling you can't go anywhere. You're trapped! The illusion of barrierlessness is inverted.

That's the perception of more than one midlifer in leadership. The freshness is gone; the fears of mediocrity, of ineffectiveness, of being lost in the shuffle are malignant.

Midlife Leadership Crisis

Penetrate the curtain of quiet thought of many forty- and fifty-year-old leaders, and you will find this wall is a very real perception:

Where can I go? And whom can I tell that I fear I can't go anywhere? And why do I feel ashamed that I even worry about these things? Would my heroes, then and now, worry about walls? What's wrong with me?

When you get to the "Denver" of my parable, you have three choices:

1. try going back to your point of origin, "youthfulness," where the dream of no limits still exists;

2. try driving in circles, cursing the wall and moaning that it's impossible to go back, or (and this is the important possibility)

3. try going up to the wall and find the passes or tunnels that lead to a healthy, spiritually vigorous, and personally effective last forty years of life.

I'm at the point in life where I've traveled through the wall and enjoyed the process! Now I know that life in the "barrierless" days was nice—but terribly unrealistic.

No wonder that in those days older men never sought me out for wisdom and counsel. They were kind to me, listened to my sermons, and followed me when I had good ideas and enthusiasm. But now I know what they were thinking: *He's a good kid who needs to grow a little before he's ready to know our hearts.*

I took my turn driving in circles. In a moment of great personal failure and sadness, I had to drive in circles while Gail and I sought the voice of the Lord about our future—whether one actually existed or not. These were some of the darkest days of my life. But they were also days of unforgettable tenderness as God taught us some things through pain that we might not have learned otherwise.

Because God is a kind and gracious God, and because I was surrounded by some men and women who believed in restorative grace, I discovered the future up in the passes and tunnels that lead through the wall.

Growth and Grace

It was a significant day when I was hit with the question: *What kind of an old man do you want to be?* And I opted for growth and grace as my old-age lifestyle. I love the words of Tennyson in his poem "Ulysses." He imagines the old, travel-worn Ulysses brooding on what one might do for an encore after having seen the world:

Tho' much is taken, much abides; and tho'
We are not now that strength which in old days
Moved earth and heaven; that which we are, we are;
One equal temper of heroic hearts,
Made weak by time and fate, but strong in will
To strive, to seek, to find, and not to yield.

That spells it out for me—"strong in will to strive, to seek, to find, and not to yield." Here's an old man who has chosen growth for an old-aged lifestyle when other old men were opting to go to Greece's version of Florida and the shuffleboard courts.

Or perhaps I could have used Paul's words—"Though our outward man perish, yet the inward man is renewed day by day" (2 Cor. 4:16 KJV). Again, "I have fought a good fight, I have finished my course" (2 Tim. 4:7 KJV). I love the enthusiasm of Tennyson's Ulysses and Paul's feistiness.

So at midlife, I asked God for a rebirth of spirit and mind. And I found a wonderful liberation. Liberation from feeling that I always had to be right and had to please everyone's definition of orthodoxy; liberation from always having to be more successful this year than last year; liberation from fearing that some people wouldn't like me; a slow and certain liberation that said, *Be content to be a pleasure to Christ, a lover to your wife, a grandfather to your children's children, a friend to those who want to share life with you, and a servant to your generation.*

28

In part, that liberation came from the grace and kindness of Jesus and also from having to clean up after failure. Those who knew me now knew my worst moments, my most embarrassing failures. I was free now to open my life and be what I was: a sinner who survives only because of the charity of Christ.

Now there is freedom to talk about fears, doubts, disappointments, and weaknesses. Because anything good that comes from someone like me actually comes from God. Paul said it best: "When I am weak, then I am strong" (2 Cor. 12:10 KJV).

Defining My Mission

I continued to wrestle with the question, *What sort of an old man do you want to be?* I looked around and discovered I didn't know many old men who impressed me with the same traits mentioned by Tennyson's Ulysses.

Why? Maybe because most men and women never build a growth plan for the old years. And if you don't plan for the kind of man (or woman) you want to be when you are eighty (God willing) and begin building that when you are forty or fifty, it's not likely to happen.

That's what drove me to define my personal mission. Without a mission, people live by reaction rather than initiation. I had written a few mission statements for organizations; why not one for myself?

Today, my mission statement sits on page two of my journal, where I read it each morning as I start my day. It defines my direction and channels my enthusiasm:

My life is focused on serving God's purposes in my generation so that the kingdom of Christ might be more firmly established wherever I go. In my dealings with people, I want to be a source of hope, encouragement, enthusiasm, friendship, and service. As a man, I seek the daily enlargement of my spirit so that it might be a dwelling place for Christ, a source of wisdom and holiness unto the Lord.

It is a functional statement, describing in broad, macro terms what I want to do with my life. It calls for me to grow by being on a constant search for the purposes of God for the times in which I live. And it puts me squarely on a mission of kingdom building: calling people to the kingdom conditions in the world in which I live.

It is a statement of quality, reminding me every day of what kind of man I want to be, what I believe Jesus has called me to be: a servant. I know the words are lofty. They are meant to be. A mission that isn't lofty isn't worth pursuing. I want my mind and spirit to be re-challenged every day with what Paul called "the high calling of God in Christ Jesus" (Phil. 3:14 KJV).

It is also a relational statement. It calls me to high standards as I interact with people, and it describes some of those standards. It outlines what I want to offer in my relationships. More than once I've awakened in a less-than-best mood and grumped a bit at Gail. And then, having successfully grumped, I have turned to my mission statement about hope, encouragement, enthusiasm, friendship, and service. Repentance usually follows.

I've heard people groan about mission statements. "Too managerial," some say. "Not my temperament," says another. "Too broad, too general, too ethereal." But I'm fascinated by a little-known instruction in Deuteronomy 17 where Moses spoke of future kings. Kings, he said, should be careful to do certain things and not do other things (such as have many wives, acquire horses, accumulate gold and silver, or send people back to Egypt).

Then, having issued that warning, Moses said this: "When he takes the throne of his kingdom, he is to write for himself on a scroll a copy of this law, taken from that of the priests. . . . It is to be with him, and he is to read it all the days of his life so that he may learn to revere the LORD his God and follow carefully all the words of this law and these decrees" (Deut. 17:18–19).

Isn't that describing a mission statement? Interesting that he would say the king should "write for himself." He is to read what he's written every day. Why? Because a king's life is open to all sorts of internal and external seductions and deceits. He needs reminders of where he's supposed to be going and what he is to avoid. Both kings and Christian leaders should construct for themselves such a statement, a covenant of growth.

My Sub-Missions

But a mission statement may not be enough. Early in this quest, I began to think about "sub-missions," equally lofty goals for each major area of my life. I identified seven areas needing discipline:

Physical: My sub-mission is to keep my body healthy, through good habits, regular exercise, prudent nutrition, and weight discipline.

Relational: My sub-mission is to love my wife in the pattern of Christ's love, to enjoy her friendship, and to make sure that her quality of life is the best I can make it. It is to be as faithful a family man as possible to my children and grandchildren. And, finally, to be a vigorous friend to a small circle of men and women to whom I'm drawn in community. Beyond that, I want to be a contributing member to my generation, always giving more to people than I take.

Intellectual: My sub-mission is to steepen my learning curve whenever possible through reading and exposure to the thinking people and disciplines of the day.

Financial: My sub-mission is to be generous, debt-free, moderate in expenditure, and careful to plan for the years of my life when income production may be difficult.

Vocational: My sub-mission is to represent the purposes of God for my generation and to teach, write, and model all aspects of "quality of spirit." I would like to make this happen both inside and outside the Christian community.

Spiritual: My sub-mission is to be a focused, holy, obedient, and reverential man before God and his world; to discipline my life so that it is controlled by the Spirit within me and so people are drawn one step closer to Christ because of me.

Recreational: My sub-mission is to seek restoration in this world by enjoying creation, caring for it, and seeking its reconciliation to the Creator.

I read these statements almost every morning as part of my personal meditations. Several comments about them:

First, they reflect what I personally think God wants from me. I don't compare myself with the apostles and the heroes anymore. Their achievements were and are unique; but so are mine. My sub-missions excite me. I seek a certain nobility in them. They motivate me to a higher way of living.

Second, they represent a variety of dreams, reflecting my life as a whole person: in touch with my body, my mind, my skills, my friends, and my world.

Third, they are flexible. Over the years, I've fine-tuned these statements as I've discovered new interests and abilities.

Finally, they are not crippling dreams. They are open-ended. They do not produce guilt when I slip backward a bit. But you can be sure that I'm sometimes chided and rebuked when I read them.

My Journal

Over the years I've introduced several other activities to my spiritual disciplines. The first and foremost is journaling. My journal carries a starting date somewhere in 1968. And since then I've managed to keep a record of almost every day of my life.

I began journaling because I discovered that many saints found it profitable. This is one of the times I copied my heroes. The saints and mystics lived without TV, phones, and all the other scintillating interruptions we've allowed into our lives. A commitment to keeping a journal forced me away from the distractions. It pressed me to think, to evaluate, to reflect, and to remember. It provided a way to look at events and impressions and interpret the presence of God in it all.

Today, I write my journal on a laptop computer, a concession to technology. It enables me to write more, do it faster, and to overcome my repugnance toward my own handwriting.

This journal becomes a tool for measuring short-term and long-term growth. The short-term measurements are daily. I frequently end a daily entry into the journal with: "Results today will be measured by _____." I list the things I believe I should accomplish and what it would take to consider those accomplishments as finished. There is a sense of well-being when I go back to that list the next day and type in "done" after each one.

Sometimes I write simple goals like "Enjoy a great afternoon with Gail," or "Review travel schedule, and make sure your calendar is up to date."

For long-term growth, I use the journal to inquire about the state of my soul. *What has Scripture been saying to me? What is God saying through my meditations? What feelings, themes, and attitudes are predominant these days? Am I fearful, preoccupied, moody, and angry? What sensitivities are being stimulated? What new thoughts or new*

33

concerns might be God's way of directing my life? This stuff has got to be written down in my world, or it just sails right through my conscious mind and leaves, having no effect.

I also use my journal approximately every four months to evaluate growth and progress. New Year's Day, my birthday (in April), and the end of vacation (August 30) are usually times to look over the past months and ask the great Sabbath questions: *Where have I been? Has the journey been fruitful? Where should I be going? Do I have the resources to get there?*

After all these words about pursuing growth, I must admit there is no guarantee against failure. Some of the very best people in biblical history failed—and terribly. What set them apart, more often than not, was not their great achievements but their repentant and broken spirits. And wasn't it a broken spirit that God said he loved best?

My Questions

Growth cannot happen when success is superficial and the heart is deceived. In the Bible, deceit was almost always challenged by the power of hard questions. To Cain: "Why is your face downcast?" (Gen. 4:6). To Hezekiah: "What have [the Babylonians] seen in your house?" (2 Kgs. 20:15 NKJV). To Judas: "Why are you here?" (cf. Matt. 26:50). To Ananias and Sapphira: "Why have you lied to the Holy Spirit?" (cf. Acts 5:3).

Gail and I have compiled some tough questions to ask ourselves when we think about growth. Questions like:

- Am I too defensive when asked questions about the use of my time and the consistency of my spiritual disciplines?

- Have I locked myself into a schedule that provides no rest or fun times with friends and family?

34

- What does my day planner say about time for study, general reading, and bodily exercise?

- What about the quality of my speech? Do I whine and complain? Am I frequently critical of people and institutions, or of those who clearly do not like me?

- Am I drawn to TV shows or entertainment that do not reflect my desired spiritual culture?

- Am I tempted to stretch the truth, enlarge numbers that are favorable to me, or tell stories that make me look good?

- Do I blame others for things that are my own fault or the result of my own choices?

- Is my spirit in a state of quiet so I can hear God speak?

In *Rebuilding Your Broken World,* I recounted the story of Matthias Rust, the young German who piloted a rental plane into the heart of the former Soviet Union and landed in Moscow's Red Square. I've always thought this to be an apt illustration of what can happen to any Christian leader at any time. The Soviets were sure they had the best systems of air defense in the world, yet a teenager penetrated their airspace and taxied up to the front door of the Kremlin. No Christ-following man or woman can feel confident that they are growing if they are not living in perpetual repentance, with a holy sorrow that acknowledges that apart from the power and grace of Christ we will succumb to the evil that abides within until the day Christ returns.

Mastering pastoral growth does not depend primarily on measuring ourselves against the saints and heroes. While there is value in learning from their lives, they are among the cloud of witnesses about whom the writer in Hebrews spoke (cf. Heb. 12:1). They remain in the stands as we run our leg of the race. We cannot match ourselves against their performances. Rather, our eyes are to be upon the One who runs with us. Thanks be to God who is alongside of us when we run, who hoists us back up when we fall, who redefines direction when we are lost, who cheers us on when we grow fatigued, and who presents us to the Father when we finish our race.

A Word of Caution

I need to go one step farther and note some things about personal growth that seem at first to be bleak. I've learned the hard way that having a mission statement, a series of sub-missions, and a process of journaling and evaluation is not a promise of success. I know failure, and I have found no human way to ensure against it.

Many years ago, I was friends with a godly older man who brought the most unusual people to Jesus. One day we were having breakfast, and Lee began to tell me about a recent trip he'd taken to Boston. "As I drove toward the city," Lee said, "I realized that I was going to be parking my car and walking through the combat zone (Boston's notorious redlight district). So I pulled into a rest stop and had a time of prayer so I could ask God to protect me from temptation when I walked past all those pornography stores and massage parlors."

"Wait a minute, Lee," I interrupted. "I don't want to offend you, but you're seventy-eight years old. Are you telling me that you're concerned about sexual temptation at your age, after all these years of following the Lord?"

Lee looked at me with an intensity. "Son, just because I'm old doesn't mean the blood doesn't flow through my veins. The difference between us old men and you young men is this: we know we're sinners. We've had plenty of experience. You kids haven't figured that out yet."

Now I understand a bit of what the old man was saying. And I understand why old men and women who are growing are among the most gracious and forgiving people there are.

Growth cannot happen without a powerful respect for the reality of indwelling evil and its insidious work through self-deceit. It leads us to lie to God, ourselves, and one another. The spiritual disciplines are designed not only to lead us into the presence of the Father but to sensitize us to the lies we can find so easy to believe.

The leader is constantly the target of temptations. We are never far from the statement King Nebuchadnezzar made on the walls of Babylon when he said, "Is not this the great Babylon I have built as the royal residence, by my mighty power and for the glory of my majesty?" (Dan. 4:30). Look around at some who have been tempted and deceived by the success of media ministry, success in fund-raising, the sensation found in fast-growing institutions, or the money capable of being accumulated through large fees and "love offerings."

The older I become the more I realize my condition as a barbarian loved by my Father. And this may be the most important insight that comes with aging. Almost all old people who are growing have certain common traits. One of them is that they know without equivocation that they are sinners. And they have come to appreciate the central importance of grace.

FOR FURTHER REFLECTION

1. *What personal barriers and limitations have you discovered in your own life that clashed with your youthful ideals?*

2. *Ask yourself the question, "What kind of old man (or woman) do I want to be?" and why.*

3. *Look at your personal mission statement, and create some sub-missions—big goals for each major area of your life. Word these in such a way that will alert you to any self-deceit that can so easily lead to temptation and downfalls.*

MAPPING YOUR INNER WORLD

*Keeping a thoughtful record of your spiritual journey can promote
godliness. It can help us in our meditation and prayer. It can
remind us of the Lord's faithfulness and work. It can help us
understand and evaluate ourselves. It can help us monitor our goals
and priorities as well as maintain other spiritual disciplines.*

DONALD WHITNEY

Journaling is such a valuable tool that I want to share more of my
own experience with it here. When I started journaling, it was because
I needed a "friend," and I wasn't doing well with the human kind. I had
passed through several weeks of high stress, the kind that young pastors
are never ready to face. I'd ignored the need for spiritual refreshment;
I'd neglected the family; I'd allowed myself to become overwhelmed
by other people's problems. There I was, one Saturday morning, crying
uncontrollably in the arms of my wife.

It was a scary moment, and it gave me a taste of the empty soul.
This must not happen again, I thought, and it came to me that writing
each day in a journal would press me to deal more forthrightly with my

emotions, with my spiritual state (or lack of it), and with the meaning of my life. I was not disappointed.

A Dialogue with the Soul

What was my journal's purpose? A journal—at least in my book—is a dialogue with the soul. It includes a record of events, but it also attempts to expose the significance of those events. *What is God saying through this? What am I learning? How do I feel? What are the principles that ooze from these events?*

Beyond that, I wanted my journal to be a story of my own journey and the journey (as much as possible) of those closest to me. The high and low points of my marriage are in my journals. Our children and grandchildren will one day be able to go back and recapture the salient events of their lives as seen through a father's eyes. They will know how much I have loved them and how proud I am of their life-choices. There are many moments when I have used my journal to pray and worship. Here and there are the indications of spiritual breakthroughs. And the journal has preserved vivid memories of the most remarkable (good and bad) moments of life.

A Journal's Possibilities

When journaling is done regularly, several things become possible:

- *The invisible and the ephemeral are forced into reality.* Once feelings, fears, and dreams are named, they can be dealt with, prayed for, and surrendered to God. They come under control, no longer existing in a way that pollutes the soul and the mind.

- *Learning experiences are preserved.* If I record and reflect on the experiences of each day, I add to my base of wisdom. Things usually forgotten or lost in the unconscious now, like books on a library shelf, wait to be tapped when parallel moments arise in the future. Now one has precedents to draw from.

- *Memories of God's great and gracious acts are preserved.* "Write this on a scroll as something to be remembered and make sure that Joshua hears it," God said to Moses after a great victory (Exod. 17:14). As Israel wandered through the wilderness and experienced God's providential care, he had them build monuments so they could remember. One day, I realized that my journal writing was a memorial to God's sufficiency.

- *I can chart areas where I need most to grow and mature.* As I look at journals from thirty years ago, I realize I have struggled with the same knot of issues throughout the years. The good news: The steps I took in the early days as I wrote of these issues turned into disciplines. And today, while issues remain, my "overcoming" rate is substantially higher. I wouldn't have spotted many of these issues if I'd not written about them day after day.

- *A journal brings dreams alive.* As ideas have flooded my mind over the years, I have written about them. Putting them into words helped me to discern the foolish ideas and develop the good ones. Many things I've done in the last few years had origins I can find in earlier journals.

FOR FURTHER REFLECTION

1. *Does the idea of a journal appeal to you? Why or why not?*

2. *If you don't have one already, begin a journal. Use it to record thoughts, prayers, and insights—and as a way to track your spiritual growth.*

3.   *If you haven't kept a journal regularly, think about developing this habit as a new spiritual discipline. After forty-five days, reflect on what you've learned from this experiment. Will you continue?*

SEARCHING YOUR MOTIVATIONS

Who is pure of heart? Only those who have surrendered their hearts completely to Jesus that he may reign in them alone. Only those whose hearts are undefiled by their own evil—and by their own virtues, too.

DIETRICH BONHOEFFER

It was a Saturday morning almost twenty-five years ago, and I had officiated in the burial of two homeless men during the past week. In both cases, I felt, their lives had been meaningless and wasted. I was overwhelmed with the sadness and emptiness of the experience.

Combined with several nights of inadequate sleep, no recent spiritual refreshment, and lots of nonstop ministry activity, their deaths left me in a state of emotional overload.

When I came to the breakfast table that morning, I had no clue I was on the brink of a crisis. Life had not yet prepared me for the fact that everyone has a breaking point. There at the table, my point came, triggered by one innocent comment.

"You haven't spent much time with the children lately," said my wife.

She was correct. I hadn't. She had kindly avoided noting that I hadn't spent adequate time with her, either. And I hadn't done any better with my heavenly Father. Added to this was the fact that work was piling up, my sermon for the next day was unprepared, and I needed to make several hospital calls. I felt like a baseball player who just bobbled the ball and the electronic scoreboard behind him begins to flash: Error! Error! Error!

Suddenly, I was engulfed with a sense of futility, and I began to cry. I lost control and wept steadily for four hours. That had never happened before. It was one of a limited number of "breaking experiences" in my life, which—more than any of the so-called successes—have been most responsible for whatever growth toward quality of soul I can claim.

What happened that day forced me to face up to something I'd either ignored or wasn't smart enough to realize: I had been engaging in ministry—supposedly in the name of Jesus—largely based on natural giftedness—my ability with words, my social skills, and my desire and energy to work for long periods of time.

Quality of Soul

That Saturday morning, I saw the first unavoidable results of a soul that lacked quality. Priorities were askew; key relationships were being neglected; my spiritual life was a joke; work was out of control. And—I mean no silliness—ministry had ceased to be fun.

When my tears dried and I had time to assess what had happened, I saw that if I were going to persevere in ministry, I was going to have to tap into deeper motivations and wellsprings of strength.

Quality of soul became my first priority. That was probably the first time I became interested in what I would later call the ordering of my private world. Other watershed experiences have come since then—some even more difficult to face—but this was the one that pressed me to ask the questions of motivation *(What was driving me?)* and maintenance *(What would keep me going?).*

That morning caused me to get serious about issues of the spirit that I'd put on the shelf for too long. In the weeks that followed, I searched my inner world. It became a rebuilding effort, a reconstruction of my base for serving God in the church.

But sometimes when you begin to rebuild, you have to first clear away some rubble. Habits, motives, illusions, ambitions, and forms of pride have to be named and renounced. This activity is called repentance. I suspect it's the most powerful exercise of the inner spirit that God has given us. It is God's weapon against deceit, which, in turn, is the most powerful weapon in the arsenal of the Evil One.

I wish I could say the personal cleanup that stemmed from that Saturday morning catharsis occurred in a short time and never had to be readdressed. But I'd speak as a fool. All that really happened was that I went on full alert to what might be the core problem of most men and women who have a heart to serve God.

It was that experience that initiated my own discipline of journaling, which I've maintained to this day. I began to discover the benefit of recording the thoughts and insights I felt God commending to my soul.

Searching the Motivation Base

What I began to see in those earliest days of private-world activity was that I had to be ruthless in dealing with my motivation base for following and serving Jesus Christ. I'm not sure I had ever given the root motivations in my life the attention they needed. My days in college and seminary, and even the first years in the pastorate ministry, had been colored with a sense of idealism, even glamour, about ministry.

The pastor's life, I thought with a mixture of naiveté and unbounded enthusiasm, would be one of changing history, building a great church, making a difference in everyone's life, preaching with fervor to people eager to hear, and enjoying a revered position as everyone's spiritual director and mentor. And if that's what the pastor's life was, then I wanted in.

But *why* did I want in? Few questions ascend in importance above that one. But only a sharp dose of reality—usually painful reality—will force us to look deeply at our motivations. The story of Simon the magician in Acts 8 is instructive. When this man saw Peter and others act in the power of the Holy Spirit, he was prepared to pay good money to have that ability.

I see a little of Simon's spirit in me. While I wouldn't be so brash as to pay money for the giftedness that makes ministry possible, at times I've succumbed to the temptation of paying for greater popularity and effectiveness by jeopardizing my health, sacrificing relationships, and otherwise burning myself out. I suspect that possibility exists in each of us.

Peter instantly challenged Simon's motivation base: "You have no part or share in this ministry, because your heart is not right before God. Repent of this wickedness and pray to the Lord. Perhaps he will forgive you for having such a thought in your heart. For I see that you are full of bitterness and captive to sin" (Acts 8:21–23).

When I search my menu of motives, I find several that are not made by God. And when I've gotten into the private worlds of other colleagues, I've discovered that I'm not alone. What follows is a partial list of substandard motives.

The Need for Approval

Paul talks a lot about our need for approval. He is unashamed to admit his desire for the approval of the "righteous judge." He is definitely out to hear God's "well done." But I'm impressed by his note to the Corinthians telling them that their approval—and even his own self-approval—is of no consequence to him. Only God's approval counts.

I compare myself with that standard and grow uneasy. Until I was eighteen, I can't remember ever considering any other profession but ministry. But the need for a wrong kind of approval may have been a major factor.

"There is no higher calling than to preach the Gospel," my mother would say to me as a child. She would add, "Now, I'm not pressuring you to do that, of course. I'd never want you to preach unless God called you to do so."

Despite her disclaimers, I interpreted the message as "Mother will be most proud and will love me most if I'm a preacher of the Gospel."

Add to that a story or two I heard regularly about my days as an infant—a story, for example, about a grandmother and a mother who laid hands on my newborn body and willed my life to preaching.

There was another story about two planes that collided above our home when I was two years old, showering our backyard with debris that should have killed me but didn't. A third story was told about my near drowning at age three and being rescued at the last second by someone who pulled me out of the water by my hair.

These stories, often retold, had a powerful effect upon my sense of direction. "God has protected you for a purpose," was the message mediated to me. "Find out what that intention is, and don't defy it."

I want to be respectful about the notion of God's special calling. But perhaps you can see why these experiences could become twisted into another process. Obeying God is one thing. Trying to please a mother, or wanting a father to be proud of you, is another. These motivations can get interwoven in the soul early in life. Then they get woven into the fabric of a sense of call, and it becomes very difficult to separate the two.

I came to see the obvious: approval from a parent or significant other can never navigate us through the often stormy waters of ministry. If we are driven by the need to hear the "well done" from human beings, even parents, we get maneuvered into something like an addiction. A certain amount of approval needed this year will, like a drug, need to be increased next year. We wind up needing more and more approval as time passes to keep up the same drive.

And since people's approval inevitably comes and goes, increases and evaporates, motivation through approval becomes a yo-yo of emotions. It's one of the first reasons men and women quit spiritual leadership. No one is clapping anymore.

Want a contrast to Simon and his evil motives? It's John the Baptist, who one day watched a formerly approving crowd leave him to follow Jesus. His reaction? "I must decrease" (John 3:30 KJV). Only a person free of the need for approval could talk like that.

Validation from Achievement

Most of us have grown up in a system highly influenced by the ethic of achievement. And the message seems clear: Those who are successful have been clearly visited with the hand of God. The corollary is likewise clear: those who are wildly successful—more so than others— have been visited with the special hand of God.

Success is usually measured in the founding or the developing of great institutions or large followings. In evangelism, it means drawing the largest crowds. In church leadership, it means heading the largest church in the region. In other ministries, it means leading the fastest growing organization (in terms of income, staff, and influence). In the publishing world, it means producing the best sellers.

When we hear Christians praise these "winners," many of us are tempted to hear that "my value" will be substantiated only when I am equally successful. And if I am not hearing this kind of praise, then maybe I am not as valuable to God as I was meant to be.

Perhaps the most dramatic statement of achievement motivation was what reputedly was said to evangelist D. L. Moody (and countless others): "The world has yet to see what God can do with one man who is totally yielded to his will."

I know many bewildered men and women who have tried their hardest to fulfill the spirit of that statement. They set out to serve God believing they are totally "yielded." But neither they nor the world ever saw any great results. They thus live in perpetual disillusionment, wondering why their faith, their labor, their commitment was not good enough to produce the results others have gained.

I recall the words of a chapel speaker during my seminary days who confused us by saying, "Don't aspire to high leadership unless it is thrust upon you." At the time that didn't make sense to me, especially since we students were constantly being told in subtle (and not so subtle) ways that the successful leader is clearly a person upon whom God's pleasure rests.

So I, like others, fantasized about pastoring a large church. And by the time I was in my mid-thirties, I'd been "blessed" with the fulfillment of that dream. But then I knew what the chapel speaker meant: there is little joy or prolonged satisfaction in high leadership if achievement is your motivation.

I discovered in those days that leadership made physical, spiritual, and emotional demands that I'd never anticipated. And without a disciplined spirit, I simply wouldn't have the reserves to go the distance. It's possible that our seminary professors told us that, but if they did, a lot of us didn't get the message. Apparently every generation has to learn the lesson the same way—the hard way.

The Bible gives us a lot of disproportionate insights. Think, for example, of all the pages devoted to the championship performances of Paul and Daniel and Moses and Esther. One evangelized his world; another served three kings with honor and bravery; a third built a nation; a fourth rescued her generation from a holocaust.

Then we read of another, Enoch, of whom it is simply said, "Enoch walked with God; then he was no more, because God took him away" (Gen. 5:24). Not much detail; no accolades; no achievements of record. But one nevertheless gets the feeling that Enoch is the equal of all the others, if not their superior.

The Longing for Intimacy

Those who study temperament styles of people know that a certain percentage of the population is driven by intimacy: the desire to connect closely with people.

There are some who love to make things or draw things or throw things or think about things. But men and women in ministry are usually disinterested in things. They're drawn to people. They want to understand them, motivate them, encourage them, and probably change them.

Put them into a room of people, and ministry people are suddenly feeling all the pain, the possibilities, the problems, and the passions that are there. They want to connect with it all, bringing meaning or healing or modification to it. That, in good measure, is the typical pastoral temperament.

The pastoral life offers great opportunity to the person who enjoys intimacy with other human beings. Properly directed, it is one of the most powerful gifts there is. Improperly directed, it leads to manipulation, exploitation, and sexual sin. If one has entered the ministry simply because it is a wonderful place to meet one's need for people-connection, the results are likely to be disastrous.

I've heard more than a few midlife men talk about leaving their careers in the marketplace to enter ministry. They are prepared to shelve a work history of twenty years to go to seminary and become a pastor. Why? Because most of the time they are disillusioned with making and selling widgets; they hate the depersonalization of the marketplace; they long to stop being so lonely and get close to people. They observe pastors who appear to spend all day talking with folks, solving problems, leading and motivating, and it looks good to them.

Scan the motive base, and you usually see that the primary call to ministry may not be Christ but rather a need to assuage the sense of isolation and alienation that careerism has created.

Timothy could have been driven by this desire for intimacy. You get the feeling he liked to make people feel good. And that's why Paul has to push him to preach, to confront, to prod, to stay the course: "Remember the gift that is in you" (cf. 2 Tim. 1:6). Without Paul's challenges, Timothy possibly would have settled down to being an awfully nice guy.

The Power of Idealism

I grew up in a highly idealistic tradition. I was immersed in triumphal language. We were going to "convert the nations" and "win the world for Christ." My early heroes were spiritual giants (at least their biographers depicted them as giants) such as Hudson Taylor and George Mueller. And my generation of Christian leaders attached an almost mystical dimension to their calling. Paul's words in 1 Corinthians 9:16—"Woe to me if I do not preach the Gospel"—rested heavily upon us. More than once I heard, "If God has given you a call and you forsake that call for anything else, you're going to live in lifelong judgment."

When I first entered ministry as a youth pastor, I was filled with that idealism. I remember my first sermon and how Gail hugged me so tightly at the end of the evening. She was proud of me; *I* was proud of me. We saw only a wonderful future of doing God's work.

Then, a few months later, the sky began to fall. I realized that doing God's work, even with my best intentions, wasn't always going to be pleasant. What I had to learn was that ministry is hard work—a noble work, but hard. And it is marked with failures and disappointments, with opposition and misunderstanding. No one had succeeded in acquainting me with Paul's momentary crashes: "We were crushed and overwhelmed beyond our ability to endure, and we thought we would never live through it" (2 Cor. 1:8 NLT).

There is probably no such thing as a pure motivation. Frankly, our hearts have too much evil embedded in them. And I suspect that even the motivations originating somewhere near purity are likely to be perverted as time goes by.

Many find it easy to write off high-profile Christians who have experienced stunning failures of one kind or another. There may be some exceptions, but I am convinced that almost every one of those who have built reputations and then collapsed started with the best of motivations. They really wanted to serve God. But the best of motivations are exchangeable for less-than-best. Only the man or woman who baptizes his or her motivations every day will have any hope that things will not turn sour down the road.

I don't know why anyone ever wanted the job of an Old Testament prophet—indeed many of those who got the job weren't seeking it. Jeremiah is a case in point. He fights the call when it comes: "I cannot speak: for I am a child" (Jer. 1:6 KJV). Later on, he confesses that he'd like to run from the city and seclude himself in the countryside (I can identify with that). Jeremiah and others prompt me to think that there is some safety when you find yourself kicking against God's call every once in a while. When you do kick, the motive base gets a retesting.

These sample motivations that I've tried to list and describe are fairly typical of the things likely to drive us in our younger years. But time and struggle generally force impurities to the surface. And each time that happens, we have to decide all over again if we will purify our motives before God and other people, or, as an alternative, grow increasingly cynical about why we entered ministry in the first place.

Many men and women reach midlife and discover their motivations for ministry are inadequate. They think it is too late to change. And so they continue on. They work their hardest to fulfill the expectations of their jobs. But that's all they are likely to be doing: jobs—nice jobs, helpful jobs, honorable jobs, but *jobs*.

By the time you reach your fifties, you may have had a number of rebuilding efforts. They usually come as a result of setbacks. Here perhaps is the one place I can safely boast (as Paul did in his weaknesses). I have known several of the classic setbacks. And, as a result, I've come to learn something about restorative grace and the process of rebuilding.

Are there great and noble motives? Of course. Moses became absorbed in the suffering of his people, and God's sensitivity to suffering and bondage became his. Samuel came to understand that the people of Israel were unable to hear God's voice through the present religious establishment. He made his voice available to God. Mary, the mother of the Lord, was clearly driven by the principle of obedience and allowed herself to be the mother of the Lamb of God. These are the motives we can nourish in our own lives.

Motives Are Never Fixed

Is it healthy to be concerned about our motive base? Well, Peter was with Simon the magician; I see the prophets wrestling with it. And I see Jesus reflecting upon his motives every time he reiterates his sense of call from the Father.

Perhaps it's a function of the older years that makes one more and more wary. I now realize that the best of motives and attitudes can be twisted even after we think we've gotten them straight.

In 1981, I went to Thailand to attend a congress of evangelical leaders. I was given the honor of delivering one of the plenary addresses. I remember thinking, *Wow! Here are hundreds of Christian leaders from scores of countries, and I am one of the very, very few asked to give a talk to the whole assembly.*

It started out as a heady time, and I remember having to rethink my motives with regularity. The drive to achieve *(Hadn't I proved myself?)*, to find approval *(Wouldn't my mother be proud?)*, to connect *(These people must like me!)*, and to realize leadership goals (being a part of a world leadership was sort of an objective) were all at work. I had a lot of soul scanning and confessing to do.

Then, three days into the conference, one of the most well-known leaders chartered a boat and invited about forty of the conferees for an afternoon of quiet consultation out on the Gulf of Siam. They were going to talk about the future of evangelical Christianity in the world. I was not among the forty.

Suddenly, being one of the speakers at the conference meant nothing. I was devastated. Not being invited to that meeting on the boat left me feeling empty. And God taught me one of the most important lessons of my life: No matter how far you go or how high you think you've climbed, there will always be forty (and probably many, many more) above and beyond you.

The moment you think of the kingdom as a place to achieve, to become valuable, to connect, or to be a major player, you will quickly discover that this was never what Jesus had in mind when he said, "Follow me."

In my book *Rebuilding Your Broken World*, I recount the story of Alexander Whyte, the great Scottish preacher, who was told that an American evangelist had accused a close friend of his of not being a converted man. Whyte was instantly outraged. His speech was barely restrained as he vented his fury on his friend's accuser.

But then, when Whyte quieted down, he was told that the same evangelist had also questioned Whyte's conversion. Instantly, Whyte fell silent. Now there was no rebuttal, just an awful quietness as he buried his face in his hands. Then he looked up at the one who had brought these reports and said, "Leave me. Leave me, my friend. I must examine my heart."

I don't think there's a person in this world who remembers what I said in my speech in Thailand. It wasn't that good anyway. But I will always value that trip. There I, like Whyte, learned an important lesson: Examine your heart. Make sure you know which motivations are in control, and don't dare step into public until you've got the answer.

FOR FURTHER REFLECTION

1. *How would you define your primary motivation? How is this reflected in your daily choices?*

2. *As a leader, are you motivated by a true desire to assist others, or are there other hidden motivations that drive you?*

3. *How have your motivations changed over the years? What precipitated the change?*

EXTREME FAITH

The LORD would speak to Moses face to face,
as one speaks to a friend.

EXODUS 33:11 NLT

About seventeen hundred years ago, there was a great church leader who is now called St. Basil. After the apostles of the New Testament, he is probably one of the greatest Christian men who ever lived. Wherever he went, he made a powerful impact upon the people he engaged. Someone once said of Basil, "His words were like thunder because his life was like lightning."

How would you like someone to say that about you? Or, to put it another way, how many times have you viewed the faith of another man or woman and said something similar about them?

You may know a lot of people who profess Christian faith, who talk the "Jesus talk" with ease, who claim they've moved far along in the journey, and yet—and I don't want to sound judgmental—you would probably agree with me that there are few people who seem miles deeper or broader or higher in their quality of faith. My phrase for them is that they exhibit "extreme faith." The man or woman with extreme faith understands there is something deeper to faith than we've imagined.

You can assess people by the things about which they are curious. I ask people, "What are your top two or three curiosities in life? What are the things you are driven to know about or that you want to master?" For too many of us, our curiosities are lesser curiosities—practical, nothing-wrong-with-them, good curiosities—not the best curiosities.

When I was a young man trying to learn how to pastor a church, my interests were in subjects like management and administration and organizational dynamics. As I've gotten older, I've learned these lesser curiosities are not the things that build either a great church or a great Christian life. Extreme faith is built upon the greater curiosities, those themes that are deep, taking a lifetime to explore.

Moses: A Man of Extreme Faith

In the Old Testament book of Exodus, there is a story that concerns one of the greatest leaders of all time—Moses. He led the people of Israel out of four hundred years of slavery in Egypt. When you read about Moses, you are reading about a man of extreme faith who spent his life exploring the greater curiosities.

Exodus 33:7–11 reads:

Now Moses used to take a tent and pitch it outside the camp some distance away, calling it the "tent of meeting." Anyone inquiring of the LORD would go to the tent of meeting outside the camp. And whenever Moses went out to the tent, all the people rose and stood at the entrances to their tents, watching Moses until he entered the tent. As Moses went into the tent, the pillar of cloud would come down and stay at the entrance, while the LORD spoke with Moses. Whenever the people saw the pillar of cloud standing at the entrance to the tent, they all stood and worshiped, each at the entrance to their tent. The LORD would speak to Moses face to face, as one speaks to a friend.

You will hardly see any place in the Bible where intimacy with God is more expressively put than in that last sentence. It describes a man who had come to know God. At this point, Moses is probably in his eighty-first or eighty-second year of life. Don't despair if you're young; it takes years to develop a relationship of this nature. Moses, through eighty years of success and failure, had finally reached this point.

But when a man or woman talks with God face to face, as friend does to friend, what do they talk about? Today, most prayers go, "O Lord, make me healthy. Solve my problems. Increase my salary. Make me happy. Help me get along with my spouse or my girlfriend or my boyfriend. Make me six inches taller. Help me take off forty pounds. Get me a better job." Is that what Moses prayed about?

One way to get an answer to that question is to discover the context of these conversations. What was going on at that time?

Moses had spent his first forty years living in the Egyptian palace. A colossal failure—a murder—drove him out of town to live in the desert for the next forty years of his life. It was during those years that Moses finally learned to start listening to God, recognizing that he must do things on God's terms. That's how extreme faith begins to develop.

In his eightieth year, at the burning bush moment, God called Moses to lead the people out of Egypt. Now remember, God asked Moses to lead tens of thousands of people out of a place where they and their ancestors had lived for four hundred years. He might as well have been asked to herd cats!

You would think that these people would be glad to get out of Egypt—"Moses, anything you say"—but when multiple generations have lived as slaves, they become distrustful. They become skeptical and suspicious. They are people without a culture. They are tempted to resist authority and to complain and gripe at everything that happens.

Consider how Israel acted just after she had been set free from her Egyptian captors. When they got to the shore of the Red Sea and the Egyptian army began to pursue them, they turned against Moses and said, "You led us out here to die. Why didn't you leave us in Egypt? Life was better then."

When they later came into the desert, they complained that the food was not in plentiful supply. Every time Moses turned around, these people were angry. They were the worst kind of people for someone to have to lead.

That's what brings us to Exodus 33:1–3:

> *Then the LORD said to Moses, "Leave this place, you and the people you brought up out of Egypt, and go up to the land I promised on oath to Abraham, Isaac and Jacob, saying, 'I will give it to your descendants.' I will send an angel before you and drive out the Canaanites, Amorites, Hittites, Perizzites, Hivites, and Jebusites. Go up to the land flowing with milk and honey. But I will not go with you, because you are a stiff-necked people and I might destroy you on the way."*

Just before this chapter, Moses had returned from Mount Sinai and found the people dancing around a fire like pagans. His brother, Aaron, had said: "We thought you weren't coming back, so we've been dancing and worshiping this calf."

God was angry.

We don't like to think of God being angry, but God has righteous anger when people turn against him and flaunt his grace. So God says: "I promised you the land, but I'm not going with you."

Three Important Prayers

Here is where the man of extreme faith begins to weigh in. As Moses hears these words, he goes to the tent of meeting. He begins to pray for three things—three things that show the greater curiosities, three things that ought to be foundational pillars in your life of prayer. These are the things men and women who grow deep in Christian faith pray about. Exodus 33:12–13 says:

> Moses said to the LORD, "You have been telling me, 'Lead these people,' but you have not let me know whom you will send with me. You have said, 'I know you by name, and you have found favor with me.' If you are pleased with me, teach me your ways so I may know you and continue to find favor with you. Remember that this nation is your people."

"Lord, Teach Me Your Ways"

The key phrase in these two verses is the first of the greater curiosities. Here is Moses, a man of extreme faith, saying to God: "Teach me your ways." What does that mean?

First of all, you are asking God to teach you about his culture. Moses had spent forty years in the Egyptian culture and forty years in the desert with shepherds, Arameans, and nomads. Now he is being asked by God to lead a group of people into a new way of life. Through his prayer, Moses is saying: "I don't know enough, God. I need to get insight into your culture—how you do things, what your expectations are, what kind of people you want us to be. So, Lord, if you want me to lead these people, teach me your ways."

This prayer drives men and women to the Word of God as students because it says, "I've been immersed for the totality of my life in the ways of the world. Though not all those ways are evil or bad, I now want to absorb God's ways. I am going to reflect the character of God in my own character. I am going to absorb as much as heaven will reveal to me about its ways."

I received an email from a friend who is on his way to extreme faith. In the last year, he has experienced a few setbacks, and they've done a job on him. I think his email illustrates what's going on in Moses' prayer:

> *God has been busy working on me. I've uncovered some strongholds in my life that have to be dealt with. I have always felt I learned about God and his ways by how he changed my circumstances. I approached my relationship with him like a rock and a stream. But God has decided it's time for me to go on to Christianity 201, which is that he wants my heart to change, not the circumstances.*

That is a remarkable insight, because most of us have prayer lives in which we're asking God to alter the circumstances. This man is saying it's not the circumstances that are to change; it's his heart that is meant to change. That's what Moses is trying to say: "Lord, I've come after eighty-two years of life to understand that I must know your ways."

If you pray like that every day, you will have a new depth to your life as you concentrate on absorbing the culture of heaven. Maybe this is part of what Jesus was saying in the Lord's Prayer: "Thy will be done on earth as it is in heaven." In other words: "I want to know your ways, Lord. I want to bring them on earth as they are explored and acted out in heaven."

"Lord, Guarantee to Me Your Presence"

The Lord says in verse 14, "My presence will go with you." Here's a change! God said earlier (in v. 3), "I will not go with you." Now, in verse 14, he apparently likes Moses' attitude. It's as if he says: "I've changed my mind. My presence will go with you."

Moses then says: "If your presence does not go with us, do not send us up from here. How will anyone know that you are pleased with me and with your people unless you go with us? What else will distinguish me and your people from all the other people on the face of the earth?"

The key idea in this part of the prayer is "Guarantee to me your presence." Moses is saying: "I'm not going to do this alone. I want to know you are where I can call upon you. I'm not going on this journey unless your presence is guaranteed."

Presence implies guidance. Presence implies help. Presence implies companionship. When my daughter, Christy, was a child, she went through a ritual each night before she went to bed. Along the baseboard of her bed were seventeen stuffed animals. The animal in the number one position got to sleep with her. The next morning, it was put in the number seventeen position and had to work its way up again. Christy was sensitive about this. More than once, I tried to slip animal twelve or fifteen to the front of the line. She always caught me, saying, "No, Daddy—number one would feel bad if he lost his turn."

The second thing in this ritual was that the sheets and blankets had to be pulled up to her chin. Then the window shade had to be pulled to six inches above the sill, no farther away and no closer. After prayers, as I went out the door, I had to shut the door to a space of about four inches, so ambient light from the hallway could come in.

Then there was a final exchange, exactly the same each night. As I slipped out the door, I would hear her say, "Daddy, where will you be?"

"Well, honey," I would reply, "I'll be with Mom in the kitchen, or in the living room, or down in my study."

And then this final comment: "Daddy, don't go to sleep until I'm asleep."

What was she saying? "I want to know about your presence. I want to know that if the night gets scary, if I hear a noise or have a bad dream, you will hear my voice."

That's what Moses is saying in this part of his prayer. While most of us may not be afraid of the dark, we have our own bag of fears. Whether it's losing our job, losing our health, not being loved, not overcoming depression, or any of the issues that create crisis in human experience, we too are crying out for the Lord's guaranteed presence.

"Lord, Show Me Your Glory"

A man of extreme faith prays a third prayer. It comes in verse 18:

Then Moses said, "Now show me your glory." And the LORD said to Moses, "I will cause all my goodness to pass in front of you, and I will proclaim my name, the LORD, in your presence. I will have mercy on whom I will have mercy, and I will have compassion on whom I will have compassion."

This is a powerful third prayer. The word *glory* is a religious word we don't often use. It sums up the worth and power of a person—or an organization, or a nation. When the president wants to impress some two-bit dictator in another part of the world, a fleet of jets will swoop down on the dictator's palace, and the sonic boom expresses the glory of the United States. When the CEO of a Fortune 500 company goes to Wall Street to impress the stock people with the glory of his or her company, he or she pulls out the figures and shows the assets, the business plans, and anything else that displays the glory of the organization.

How does God reveal his glory to Moses? God says: "I'll tell you what my name is. I will reveal something to you of my moral character. Here is my glory, Moses: I am abounding in steadfast love, slow to anger, and forgiving of wickedness and sin. I am not capricious, vindictive, or unresponsive. I am a God whose character is impeccable and absolutely dependable."

Time to Go Deeper

Let's say you are Moses, and you've been asked to take a recalcitrant group of people across a desert to the Promised Land, and you don't know whether you've got it in you. The moment calls for the development of extreme faith.

Can you do it on the kind of prayers most of us pray? Probably not. But if your prayers become studded with prayers like "Teach me your ways," "Guarantee to me your presence," and "Show me your glory," your faith is going to enlarge.

In the seventh and eighth centuries, Christianity virtually died out in Europe. The only place where Christianity was of any influence was in Ireland, where Irish monks preached the faith. These Irish monks did some interesting things to express their extreme faith. Many of them would get into little boats and put out into the sea, trusting that wherever the current led them was where God wanted them to go. Many of them perished, but those who landed on the shores of the European continent preached the Gospel. Today, you can still find great monasteries that were founded by Irish monks in that period of time. In fact, an Irish monk founded the monastery where St. Francis of Assisi experienced his conversion.

One of the greatest Irish monks was St. Brendan. Before he embarked upon the seas, he is said to have prayed this prayer:

Shall I abandon, O King of mysteries, the soft comforts of home? Shall I turn my back on my native land and my face toward the sea? Shall I put myself wholly at the mercy of God, without silver, without a horse, without fame and honor? Shall I throw myself wholly upon the King of kings without a sword and shield, without food and drink, without a bed to lie on? Shall I say farewell to my beautiful land, placing myself under Christ's yoke? Shall I pour out my heart to him, confessing my manifold sins and begging forgiveness, tears streaming down my face?

Shall I leave the prints of my knees on the sandy beach, a record of my final prayer in my native land? Shall I then suffer every kind of wound that the seas inflict? Shall I take my tiny boat across the wide sparkling ocean? O King of the glorified heaven, shall I go of my own choice upon the sea? O Christ, will you help me on the wild waves?

You and I may not be as articulate as St. Brendan, but more than a few of us are right where he once was. We're on the beach. We've done Christianity 101. We've had a prayer life that depended upon changing circumstances. God is now saying, "I want to take you deeper."

You might be saying, "I want to go deeper; I want to be a person of extreme faith. Where do I start?"

You start where Moses started. On his own beach, as he faced God with incredible challenges in front of him, he prayed a powerful three-fold prayer:

Lord, teach me your ways. Guarantee to me your presence. Show me the revelation of your power and your glory.

Those are the greater curiosities. This is the prayer of a man or woman who wants to develop extreme faith.

FOR FURTHER REFLECTION

1.   *What typically do you pray about? How much of your focus is on solving your problems or increasing your paycheck, and how much is focused on deepening your intimacy with God?*

2.   *How would you define your own faith? Is it lukewarm, faltering, or extreme?*

3.   *As a way to become a person of extreme faith, try praying Moses' threefold prayer on a daily basis. Jot down in your journal any results you notice.*

THE ROOT OF LEADERSHIP

*May your roots go down deep into the soil of God's
marvelous love. . . . Then you will be filled with the
fullness of life and power that comes from God.*

EPHESIANS 3:17–19 NLT

Gail and I had a chance to visit Yosemite National Park in California. We brought home pictures of us standing at the foot of some of those three-thousand-year-old trees that rise a zillion feet into the air. Think of it—three thousand years to grow a tree. And think again—given modern machinery, the same tree can be (perish the thought!) cut down in just a few minutes.

Those trees prompted a thought about leadership and the issue of trust, the kind of trust leaders desperately need from their people but sometimes do not possess.

No biblical leader that I can think of struggled with trust issues more than Moses. Every time the man turned around, someone was questioning his judgment, his veracity, and his sense of direction. You could argue that they finally broke him with their patterns of suspicion and defiance.

The apostle Paul cashed in on trust when he asked people to give him money to aid in the relief of suffering Christians in Jerusalem. He must have leaned on the trust factor when he convinced Timothy's family to release him to mentorship.

Trust was in play when Paul gave strict orders to the Corinthians to discipline a known sinner. And—trust again—when he convinced them to take the man, now repentant, back. Trust won the day with Philemon, who was asked to receive a runaway slave back into his home—no longer as a slave but as a brother. No doubt about it: Paul's word in most places was like gold. Trust backed that currency.

I learned quickly in my youngest pastoral years that people would follow only so far if I traded exclusively on my natural gifts: words that came easily, personal charm, new ideas, and dreams. I was tempted to think that just because I had a seminary degree, because I was ordained, and because I was more knowledgeable about biblical ideas, people should have unlimited faith in me.

That stuff works for a while, but in crunch time deeper questions begin to emerge. *Did I have integrity and wisdom, or was it all froth? Was I reliable? Could I take people into unknown territory spiritually and organizationally?* Charm and charisma are like a glider; they fly, but not indefinitely. And they don't do well in turbulent times.

Crunch time might come when a leader asks people to come up with a staggering amount of money for a building, a staff addition, or a project of generosity that benefits the poor. Crunch time might come when people are asked to abandon an old program and embrace something entirely new. Or it might happen when a leader has to confront a blind spot or hardened spirit about something that requires repentance and new direction.

Trust in Personal Encounters

More important—over the long haul—is how trust comes into play in the personal encounters of pastoral life.

Years ago, I had the privilege of leading a young man to faith in Jesus. At the time, he was living with a girl who was the daughter of one of our church leaders. Her family had despaired that she (or he) would ever walk in biblical light. Then one Sunday (for reasons I have forgotten), the two of them came to worship. At the end of the service, I met this couple, conversed with them, and eventually witnessed this young man's conversion and change of life.

The young woman, raised in faith but obviously drifting, came back to spiritual life as a result. It wasn't long before the two of them—recognizing the importance of biblical obedience—asked if I would marry them. I was delighted.

Then they cautioned me. Her father and mother, they said, would likely be hostile to their marriage. On behalf of the couple, I would have to approach the parents and gain their permission. I agreed to do this.

I recall sitting in the living room of this long-time Christian mother and father. The drama of the moment is such that even now, many years later, I can recreate my words to them. Calling them by name, I said, "I'm going to ask you to trust me. It is my judgment that your daughter and her boyfriend should marry. I believe that he is ready to be a loving and responsible husband and that she is prepared to assume the disciplines of marriage. I want you to support their desire to get married."

There was a short, quiet pause as the parents took this in. Then the father said these words: "Pastor, we trust you. And if you think they are ready to be married, that this is a good decision, then we'll give them our blessing." And they did.

This couple has now been married for more than twenty-five years, and the judgment we all made has been vindicated over and over. It would not have happened, however, if I had not been able to trade on trust.

Earned Trust

The great Victorian physician Sir William Osler once said to his medical students:

> *The practice of medicine is an art, not a trade; a calling, not a business; a calling in which your heart will be exercised equally with your head. Often the best part of your work will have nothing to do with potions and powders, but with the exercise of an influence of the strong upon the weak, of the righteous upon the wicked, of the wise upon the foolish. To you, as the trusted family counselor, the father will come with his anxieties, the mother with her hidden grief, the daughter with her trials, and the son with his follies. Fully one-third of the work you do will be entered in other books than yours.*

With very little change in wording, Osler could have been talking to those in pastoral ministry. Trust makes possible "an exercise of influence." Oh, by the way, trust makes it possible to fail occasionally. People forgive a failing moment if their overall perspective is of great trust.

I have been impressed with the new breed of leaders who have a passion to launch great church-based evangelistic endeavors. I admire them, and I value their friendship. They certainly have surpassed anything I (or most pastors in my generation) could have dreamed. And they write well about the skill sets of leadership: things like vision, passion, cultural sensitivity, developing leaders, and lots of other things.

There is one thing, however, I don't hear enough about, and that may reflect a tendency to think that leadership is mostly about skill and instinct. What don't I hear about is trust, that almost indescribable quality of relationship in which a leader builds and then enjoys the confidence of the people.

"We make our money the old-fashioned way," the Smith-Barney company once declared in its commercials. "We earn it!" Similarly, one gains trust the old-fashioned way: it is earned. It cannot be demanded or assumed.

One of my theories has been that a leader really does not begin to enjoy the leadership "bite" or "traction" that is necessary to get things done until he or she has been leading for about five years. Therefore, the fifth year and beyond are years where trust is all important because novelty and newness no longer exist. As my father used to remind me, people will follow you for a while because they picked you. But they'll follow you over the long term because they have learned to trust you.

Back to the gigantic trees in California: they are not hard to cut down in a short period of time. Like them, trust can be forfeited in a short amount of time. I know. I once forfeited the trust of people I cared for very much. I lost some very precious friendships. And I lost my honor. To regain any of what was lost took a long time.

How to Build Trust

Now comes the big question: How is trust generated? Here are seven sources I have observed over the years.

1. Trust builds with consistency. Consistency of message, of vision, of the management of circumstances. People are constantly watching. They want to know: Will you be the same person when things are going wrong? Can you hear a thoughtful "no" from the board? Will your personal responses be in alignment with the things you have preached from the safety of the pulpit?

2. Trust builds with dependability. Are you a person of your word? If you make an appointment, are you there on time? If you commit to doing something for someone, does it get done as promised? If you make a promise, make sure it is kept.

3. Trust builds with openness. Are you truthful about yourself? Are you honest about what is really happening behind the scenes of the organization? In trustworthy people, there is an absence of slickness, slogans, and strategies that do not offer the full message. People do not feel tricked or duped.

4. Trust builds with a reputation for hard work. Sermons reveal a craftsmanship of serious study. The pastor gives the congregation just a bit more than what it thought it paid for. Board and committee meetings are marked with thoughtful presentations and explanations. There is a sense that the pastor is on top of the job of congregational leadership.

5. Trust builds with a belief that the pastor has an impartial pastoral eye for everyone. The rich (major donors), the attractive, the young, or the influential are not uniquely favored. The pastor engages with the children, with the weak and the struggling, with the old, and with the more common person who serves in the congregation in places where recognition is scarce.

6. Trust builds with longevity. This simply means that the pastor hangs in there for an extended time. Relationships are built; the buildup of ministry episodes (funerals, weddings, baptisms, etc.) occurs; people see the pastor sharing their passages of life. And when that crunch time comes, they are more apt to say, "The pastor was there for me; I'll be there for what he believes God wants for us now."

7. Trust builds with an ever-deepening spirit. Somehow the congregation wants to feel that their pastor fixes his or her eyes on Jesus. They gather confidence when they sense that the pastor's life and leadership reflect a person who seeks the heart of the Father and speaks out of a certitude that is humble yet convinced, fully repentant yet graced, self-effacing yet competent through the power of God.

More than once I asked my congregation for second offerings which would be given to people in some part of the world who had sustained a great tragedy. Trust made it possible for people to dig deep. More than once I asked my congregation to step out in faith on a new budget or building program or staff addition. Trust made them willing to do it.

And more than once I asked my congregation to swallow hard and accept something that was new or even went against the grain of their instincts. Only trust made this possible.

Trust eludes a complete definition. But, as they say, you know it when you see it. And I think about that when I look skyward at an enormous California sequoia. How long to grow; how quickly destroyed.

FOR FURTHER REFLECTION

1. *Who are some of the trustworthy leaders in your own life? What effect did being able to trust them have on your life? Have you also encountered untrustworthy leaders? What impact did this have on you?*

2. *Has there been a time in your life when you lost the trust of someone you valued? What were the circumstances, and were you able to regain it? If so, how?*

3. *As a leader, how do you inspire trust and confidence in the people God has entrusted to you?*

MONDAY MORNING RESTORATION

I must secure more time for private devotions.
I have been living far too public for me. The shortening
of devotions starves the soul, it grows lean and
faint. I have been keeping too late hours.

WILLIAM WILBERFORCE

Monday morning. In the past seventy-two hours, I have given five sermons, prayed and talked individually with at least twenty-five people in need of some sort of spiritual change, listened to the complaints of two "hurt" people, and chatted with a couple whose marriage is unraveling.

I am tired, feeling uncertain, and irritated that I didn't do better yesterday. In the next forty-eight hours, my datebook says I will have

- attended a major staff meeting

- spent an evening with several dozen new members

- had breakfast with one of our elders

- visited with a distraught wife whose husband is depressed

- lunched with a pastor who wants to talk about how to develop visionary leaders

- met with an older couple who are desperately lonely because most of their friends have died or gone to Florida

- "dinnered" with members of our pastoral team who want to propose some dreams about the future.

Interspersed among these hours will be finishing an article, a first glance at next weekend's preaching material, and responding to about thirty emails.

Obviously, I've not said anything about private time with my wife, conversations with my grandchildren (who will definitely call), and some badly needed introverted moments for myself.

In the midst of all this, I am expected (by myself and others) to be a spiritually passionate person! By that, I mean a person who evidences a touch of wisdom, grace, power, and faith (words that characterized Stephen in Acts 6) and makes it available to others. Without those qualities of spirit, my effectiveness as a pastor quickly sags.

Yet I feel I am constantly on spiritual discharge with precious little time to refill. I've never forgotten Jesus' words to Simon Peter when the disciple was incredulous that the Lord was asking, "Who touched me?" while in the middle of a crowd. "I know that power has gone out from me" (Luke 8:45–46).

The acquisition, maintenance, and siphoning off of spiritual energy is the chief concern of pastors who want to stay vital. The long-range result of running on empty is horrific: becoming bitter-spirited, reduced to going through the motions; falling into ministry-destroying sin; losing intimacy with God and spouses and friends; and (if nothing else) hating our work.

As Ruth Graham once said when asked if she'd ever thought of divorcing Billy: "Divorce? Never! Murder, several times," I think about ministry: *Quit? Never! Run away to Switzerland and climb mountains? Every Monday!*

Refreshing the Spirit

How does a leader refresh his or her spirit? What little I know about the freshening of the inner spirit, I've learned the hard way, mostly through failures, dry times, the awful moments when I knew I had to speak into the souls of people but had virtually nothing to offer.

I've rarely lacked words, ideas, or a glad hand for people. But I haven't always had the "right stuff" that comes only from the depth of a filled soul. Here are a few ideas that have made my Monday mornings more manageable.

Acknowledge My Sinfulness

In the past, I've tried to act, speak, and impress people as if I were a reincarnation of Oswald Chambers. I sometimes tried to select the correct spiritual-sounding responses, pray prayers that sounded "godly," and engage in the double-talk of false modesty. I wonder if I appeared as ridiculous as I felt.

One day, it became apparent that I had the capacity to be a terrible sinner, and the cat was out of the bag. St. Paul and I had a similar problem: sinfulness. I am a sinner who makes many return trips to the cross for forgiveness and restoration. So why not acknowledge it and get on to delighting in God's mercy?

I have learned to be quick to acknowledge my sinfulness to others. Paul's self-disclosure that he was "the worst of sinners" (1 Tim. 1:16) is a good start as a public declaration.

Downsize My Word Output

Few leaders know how to ask questions of others, how to seek what God may be saying in other people's experiences. Our instinct too often is to speak of everything we know, as if doing so is the only way to authenticate ourselves.

I have been working hard to stop telling people my latest insights, my spiritual intentions, and my opinions about every leader, every organization, and every ministry. I'm not quite as smart or wise as I used to be (he says, tongue-in-cheek), and I'm finding that saying less is better. Talking too quickly, too much, and too cleverly is destructive to the spirit. The spiritual men and women I've come to admire were generally quiet-spirited and more silent than verbose.

This is hard for those of us who are extravagantly verbal. But I have driven myself to become more of a question-asker and less of an answer-giver. I have come to appreciate the wisdom of Brigid Hermann who once observed that the more we talk to others about all we are learning and experiencing, the less we need to talk to God.

Map Each Day

I now map each day according to a purpose. In the front of my journal is "my daily intention," which describes what significant living means to me. My daily intention has been forged out of much meditation, prayer, and experimentation. Like the banks of a river, it helps me to channel my energies in the right direction.

For example, my daily intention speaks of cheerful and reverent communion with the Father, cooperation and devotion in community with those I love, and pastoral and humble commitment to service in Christ's kingdom. Each morning, through this threefold lens, I meditate on the day in front of me. It provides shape for my prayers, a basis for my meditative reading, and a check on my personal planning.

Reconceive God's Love

In my younger years, my love for God was based on a sentimental or romantic model. No wonder I had trouble finding much reality in it—or even sustaining it. My love for God is now much better perceived on a father/son model. It is an adventure in understanding how to honor God; to reverence, obey, and thank him; to express appropriate sorrow for blunders and sin; and to pursue a "shyness" in which I might hear him whisper into my soul.

These are not the activities of a romantic relationship; they make better sense only when I come to God as the divine parent.

Get My Hands Dirty

As strange as it may sound, I have found that one key to spirituality is participating in the common work of my home and marriage. For too many years, I gave the management and maintenance of our home, our social calendar, our finances, and our personal life (laundry, cooking, etc.) to my wife so I could maximize my efforts in the "big stuff." People in leadership positions (particularly men) have a tendency to slough off the simple work of a home.

But in such work, a portal to genuine humility is found. Humility is not acquired by being modest; it is found in embracing the simple matters of ordinary work. The monastics have known this for centuries.

Not only will I take out the garbage or clean a bathroom because I'm asked, I assume such chores as an ongoing responsibility. I find much of God's presence (and an upgrade of respect from my wife) in doing the simple things.

Renounce Fixing as a Way of Life

I now reject what I feel is the superficial intensity of much Christian ministry: that everything is a problem, that every person needs to be fixed, and that all the work of the kingdom has to be done by the time I die. Ministry is my life, but I am no longer reluctant to make sure there is fun in my calendar (with Gail and with carefully cultivated friends). I laugh a lot more now and make sure my enthusiasm for life is high every day.

In my conversations with pastors, I am dismayed at how many have put their personal desires on hold. That can build a pit of anger and personal sadness. As a young husband and father, I gave up skiing for other priorities. But later in life, my wife encouraged me to return to the slopes. Now, a high point of my year comes with a couple of days in the Rockies. I'm the first one on the lift in the morning and the last one still on it in the late afternoon. I've learned to play again.

In addition, I no longer have to be right every time I open my mouth. I no longer have to be the best, no longer have to control every situation, no longer have to be at every national function of pastors and Christian leaders, and no longer have to offer an opinion or endorsement on every dream, vision, and movement that someone feels God has called him or her to launch. I have actually learned to say no. I don't have to market myself, sell myself, or offer myself.

Spend Time with the Weak

I used to try to spend all of my time with the strong. I was urged to prioritize my time. Even now, the organizational leader in me says, "Spend time with the folks with the big bucks, the political instincts, the best connections, and the charisma." Then one day I became one of the weak, and I learned what it was like when several came alongside for no better reason than to assure me they loved me. As a result, I have tried hard to learn how to become a friend to the weak.

The weak are not necessarily people with problems; they are rather the "unnoticed": the very old, the very young, the socially awkward people. At one of our Wednesday night gatherings at Grace Chapel, I asked a young mother if I could hold her baby while she went through a serving line and enjoyed a brief meal with her husband and friends. The baby and I got along famously, and the mom and dad seemed touched by the fact that a pastor had affection for their most-beloved child.

The old, the deeply repentant, the pained, and the children know a lot more about reality than the strong. I've discovered that the weak say some of the most fascinating things. Perhaps that's because God spends most of his time, according to Isaiah 57:15, with the "contrite and lowly in spirit."

Come to the Quiet

Going to bed early most evenings has afforded me the chance to seize early morning hours before calls, emails, and appointments begin their relentless intrusion. In the quietness, the Scriptures, ancient liturgies, prayers, and the spiritual reflections of the masters have informed my soul. I have come to love the Bible all over again—and with it the reflections of the ancients and not-so-ancients from a score of traditions.

Spiritual Passion Refound

Someday, after I have left this place, my children will have a problem: what to do all the years of journals that tell my story of ups and downs, achievements and humiliations. If they choose to read snippets here and there, they will come to see how ordinary a man I was, but how kind God has been in these quiet moments to fill the empty spaces with his promises and affirmations.

Such spiritual quests are not a guarantee against failure or defeat. But if they become habitual, they offer a place to go, a form to follow in the moment of defeat.

So, on this Monday morning after a wild weekend of activity, I come to my private altar with my Bible, my reflective literature, my laptop, and my near-empty soul. I've been here before. God has something to say to this tired soul. And when he's finished, I'll be a reasonably new man again. Spiritual passion refound.

FOR FURTHER REFLECTION

1. *In your life, what are the events, activities, people, or trigger points that push you to the point of exhaustion?*

2. *How has the way you perceive your relationship with God changed over the years? Do you perceive him as your Father?*

3. *How do you personally create the refreshment you require to recharge your batteries and lead with energy? Are there hobbies or activities that you've neglected, and if so, how could you incorporate them into your life again?*

THE PRIVATE TIMES
OF A PUBLIC LEADER

Though I am always in a haste, I am never in a hurry,
because I never undertake more work than I can
go through with perfect calmness of spirit.

JOHN WESLEY

In Walter Trobisch's delightful book *I Married You* there is a record of intense conversation between the author and the wife of Daniel, an African pastor. Walter and Esther are seated at the dining room table in her home waiting for Daniel to join them following a Sunday morning service in which Walter has given a talk on marriage. Now they sit before a magnificent dinner prepared by Esther.

But the problem is Daniel. He isn't there. And that fact increasingly irritates Esther, who is aware that her husband is just outside conversing with lingering church members. He seems oblivious that he is ignoring their guest and offending an upset wife who has done her best to provide genuine hospitality.

Unable to ignore the signs of her frustration, Walter says to Esther, "You suffer, and you are embarrassed because of me." After gaining her composure, Esther responds, "I love Daniel very much, but he is not a man of schedule. I don't mind hard work, but I want to plan my day and have order in my duties. He is a man who acts out of the spur of the moment. He is an excellent pastor. People like him very much, but I'm afraid they take advantage of him too."

At the base of Esther's concern is the problem of time. She and Daniel disagree on how to properly use it. And the result? They are becoming increasingly ineffective in doing the things to which they were originally committed, and the time problem is beginning to have a corrosive effect on their marriage relationship.

Properly understood and managed, time is easily one of our best friends. Poorly appreciated and mismanaged, it becomes a formidable enemy. Peter Drucker, among others, has made it quite plain that the issue of time is at the very base of one's effectiveness as a leader and manager. In his book, *The Effective Executive,* he is careful to remind us that time is *inelastic*—it can't be stretched; *irreplaceable*—it can't be reclaimed; and *indispensable*—things cannot be done without it.

The earthly ministry of Jesus Christ points up some helpful principles about the general use of time. It is nothing new to point out that Christ never showed signs of being hurried, pressured, or playing what we call "catch-up." While he was certainly physically tired on occasion, he never appeared emotionally frustrated due to a lack of time, something we see a lot in present Christian ministry.

We read of Jesus ignoring large crowds to confer with twelve men at length. We see him sleeping in a boat, skipping a meal to talk with a woman, yet interrupting an encounter with a large number of adults to visit with children. Interesting uses of time, wouldn't you agree? Surely some must have shaken their heads about the strange ways Jesus invested the hours of his life. But, in retrospect, we see that he never missed making correct use of his time, and his mission was accomplished in just thirty-three years.

Today, many people write about burnout. Why didn't Jesus burn out? I think the answer rests in three simple principles: Jesus measured all investments of time against his purpose, he took time for solitude with the Father, and he didn't try to do too much.

Myths About Time and Leadership

We need to see through certain myths about time that we've been teaching one another for many years. Such myths are contrary to the principles Jesus employed in his ministry.

Myth #1. We are individually responsible for saving the whole world. Laugh at the absurdity of it, but many of us act as if we really believe that nonsensical statement. The source of the myth lies in our drive to match the potential we imagine God has given us. Also, we don't like to be left out of things that others are doing. So we find ourselves wanting to speak at every conference, to be a member of every board that invites us, to consult on every matter that faces our crowd, and to become friends with every luminary on our horizon.

Succumb to the myth—as many do—and the tragic end comes when, in discouragement, you learn that you never know enough people, can never attend all the conferences, and never find time for all the board meetings. Slowly we learn that we cannot save the world, but rather, we can make a dent on our world.

Myth #2. Time is running out; too little of it is left. Do I run the risk of losing some of my treasured friends in faith when I publicly depart from the ranks of those who think the "midnight hour" is upon us, and we haven't a moment to lose?

I have stopped admiring the driven man. Now my admiration increasingly targets on the person who, like the farmer, has learned patience, the one who has learned that the best things grow in time and all we can do is follow the proper sequence of planting, cultivating, and harvesting. No harvest can be enlarged by frantic hurrying about.

All my life, I have been hustled by those who predicted world destruction just around the corner. If I had responded to their predictions, I would be a wasted midlifer. Although I'm confident that world destruction or the imminent return of Christ could happen even today, I am also just as ready to perform as though another thousand years lie ahead.

Myth #3. A leader must be constantly available for all emergencies. As a young pastor, I was nursed on the notion that a call to ministry meant that my time belonged to the congregation night and day, fifty-two weeks a year. Too frequently, I heard whispered admiration for the dedicated man who never took a day off, rarely vacationed, and offered himself as instantly approachable. There was a time when I really believed in that sort of life, and I felt guilty because I resented its demands.

I still believe in reasonable accessibility as a leader. On the other hand, I am no longer afraid to be out of touch with people when it comes time for me to pursue solitude, family time, or the enjoyable moments of living in this wonderful world. In all my years of being a pastor to three congregations, I faced only a few situations in which my presence was instantly needed.

Myth #4. Rest, recreation, and leisure are second-class uses of time. Do you remember the intimidating question many of us used to be asked as young people? "If Jesus came while you were [attending a movie, kissing your girlfriend, or hanging around with the gang at the local drive-in], would you want him to find you in that situation?"

The question has a nagging way of hanging on into adulthood. It now can spring from the conscience when we ask ourselves what Jesus might think if he came and found us playing racquetball, canoeing on the Penobscot River in Maine, attending a Boston Pops concert, or, dream of dreams, watching the Boston Celtics play in the NBA playoffs.

Why is there such uneasiness about rest, recreation, and leisure? Because we have inadvertently sorted our time into good, better, and best classes. Leadership, we think, is first-class time; all other activity is second- or third-class time. Wrong! On the whole, the God of the Bible has to be just as pleased when his children play as when they work, when each is done to make possible the greater effectiveness of the other. "Come apart and rest" are the words of Christ. And "God rested and refreshed himself" are the words of Moses.

Myth #5. It is glamorous, even heroic, to burn out, break down, and even relationally blow up if you can prove that your friend or your spouse left you because you were faithfully discharging your call. Although I don't wish to diminish the saint who has given his or her life for the sake of the Gospel, it is just as right to pursue a long life of regular service that peaks in old age with a mass of wisdom and experience to be handed on to the next generation.

Myth #6. The family of the Christian leader automatically surrenders its right to spiritual and familial leadership by the father (or the mother). An earlier generation of missionaries often left its children in the care of others and went off to other parts of the world. They labored under the illusion that, if they would be faithful to ministry, God would guarantee the growth and development of their children. Tragically, a significant portion of those people found it didn't work that way.

We in Christian leadership have no business having families if we are not committed to taking care of them and raising them properly. They are not someone else's business. When I was first beginning my life as a young pastor, I once approached an older preacher and asked him, "What is more important, my family or the Lord's work?" His response has never left me: "Gordon, your family *is* the Lord's work."

The World of Private Time

A business executive says to me, "I'm alarmed at the poor quality of my time away from my work. It seems as if all I do is run to this or that church or civic meeting. I have almost no time to just sit quietly and talk to my wife, or to catch up on my own thoughts. Frankly, we're both so tired with this incessant running that even the sexual dimension of our lives is hurting. We're perpetually exhausted."

Here is a place where all leaders have a similar problem. Our work and the demands upon us seem to expand to fit all the time that we possess. As long as we permit that to happen, we will always be behind, wondering where and when it all ends.

What are some of the necessary nonwork times each of us needs?

Alone-Time

Would it be surprising if I suggested that my first need as a person is for alone-time? This includes spiritual solitude, where I can commune with God as Christ himself did, but it also includes time to think, to exercise, and to keep company with myself. When we are constantly amid the noise and rush of persons and programs, we can hardly ever brood or think, and the lack of time to do such things inhibits our growth.

With some regularity, I have built into my schedule a day alone to walk, sit, or paddle a canoe on a wilderness river. How vitally important it is to be silent for a period! In the alone-times, my mind and inner spirit become once again a fountain of ideas and possibilities. I am able to catalog the issues with which I am personally struggling, whether they are matters of faith, job, or relationship.

Naturally, this alone-time enlarges to include one's family. In our home, we believe that our marriage is itself a gift to our congregation as a model of Christian relationship. Therefore, my wife and I have understood the importance of maximizing our opportunities to commune with one another so that our relationship remains healthy and whole. We pursue alone-time, for example, on a daily basis with conversation about the events in both of our days when I return home from my study. We call this encounter our marital quiet time; and because we find it important to make it happen the minute I arrive, I usually phone my wife as I leave the office.

These same principles applied with our children as they were growing up, and we worked hard at being with them. Evening mealtimes were known as inviolable on all of our schedules, and although we all were extremely busy people, we all knew the family would rendezvous each day at supper for an hour. Incidentally, while we were together for that hour, the phone remained turned off.

Downtime

I have become aware that in my private life there is also a need for what I call downtime. None of us in leadership is without downtimes, those periods in our lives which inevitably appear soon after we've put out unusually high levels of emotional energy or brought a major effort to a conclusion. Downtimes also may occur following a highly intense period of interaction with people, when one has been drained by incessant conversation, decision-making, and advice-giving.

I suspect that there are even general downtimes during certain seasons of the year for all of us. I have found that May is a low month for me, and it seems to stem from the fact that I have been "carrying" a lot of friends and congregational members through the late winter months and into the spring. They have been having their own downtimes, and while they were down, I had to be up. May seems to be my turn.

What can be done about downtimes? Well, for one thing, we can accept them as a part of the rhythm of life. Second, we can keep them in mind when making up a schedule. If Monday mornings are depressing, then avoid scheduling commitments that drain more of what was already given on Sunday. Work or rest should fit with the generalized mood of that period. If I look at my calendar and see a ten-day period with a heavy schedule and lots of pressure, I immediately try to block off one day at the conclusion of that period so I can begin to restore the energies that will be drained during the difficult period.

The most important thing to remember about downtimes is that they are not necessarily signs of personal or spiritual immaturity. They are as essential for the mind and emotions as a pause is for a person who engages in heavy physical labor.

Sabbath-Time

Another sort of private time I regularly seek I call Sabbath-time. I love the words in Exodus concerning God and his own Sabbath time.

> *[The Sabbath] is a sign forever between me and the people of Israel that in six days the* LORD *made heaven and earth, and on the seventh day he rested and was refreshed (Exod. 31:17 ESV).*

Sunday is no Sabbath for any pastor, or for many in the lay leadership of large congregations . . . it is time that many of us in ministry grow more serious about the genius of the Sabbath experience. I see Sabbath-time as a more deliberately planned piece of time for silence, reflection, spiritual discovery, and the joyful recounting of past achievements and activities. Sabbath-time is definitely not a time for catching up on household chores, exhausting recreation, or parties. Sabbath-time is retreat, withdrawal. In it, one worships, meditates, and seeks a filled inner spirit. At its conclusion, one is refreshed.

We have strayed so far from the biblical concept of the Sabbath that one is almost stymied to describe what events should occur during such a time. I can hear someone saying that there is no time for this idealistic pursuit. If that is true, then we have overloaded our lives with more relationships, deadlines, and responsibilities than God can possibly be pleased with.

Lately, my wife and I have pursued the ideal of one day a week which we call our Sabbath. It is more than a day off; it is restoration time replete with reading and meditation. It is a day of recharging our souls so that when we come away from the "mountain" we have something to give away in terms of spiritual energy to the people whom we serve.

I am impressed with the obscure statement of John after Jesus finished speaking to the people, "Then each went to his own home. But Jesus went to the Mount of Olives" (John 7:53–8:1). Our Lord knew he had spent himself and needed a Sabbath restoration. Others went back to their noisy and people-filled routines; Christ pursued quiet, where the voice of the heavenly Father could be heard. When he returned from the mountain, he had new and fresh things to say.

Growth-Time

Pastors should pursue something else in the private sector of life, which I will call growth-time. Begin with growth-time in terms of the body, for example. For me, physical growth-time occurs between 5:00 and 6:00 A.M. several mornings each week when I run (well, to be more honest, jog) for thirty to forty-five minutes.

Usually, my mind and emotions conspire against the notion of running, and, like my prayer life, I've never found a way to automatically want to run. But once I've run for more than half the time I've allotted, I manage to convince my mind and emotions that we're really going to do this all the way and that they might as well finish the course along with my body. When we all cross the finsh line together—body, mind, and emotions—I have an amazing feeling of personal victory.

Growth-time also means exercising my mind. Each month, I try to spend a few hours at the public library to come in contact with new titles and explore the broad expanse of available knowledge which may be good for me and for my congregation.

As another means of growth-time, I have deliberately embraced a hobby in midlife, one that guarantees privacy, diversion, and mobility. For me, it is photography. For my friend John Stott, it's bird-watching. For another pastor friend of mine, it's woodworking, and for still another, antique clock repair. I like my hobby because I can take advantage of my travels to expand the range of places for taking pictures.

Growth-time also means taking on challenges that stretch one's imagination. My family and I have canoed the wildernesses of Canada and Maine. We have accumulated tremendous memories of near disaster and spiritual euphoria on those trips. They are memories which undergird all of our experiences, and we have all grown through them.

Discipline and Time

How have we maintained any sort of semblance of order to our public and private times? Several random observations about things my wife and I have learned as the years have passed may be helpful.

First, we believe in the necessity of a calendar. Gail and I have maintained a master calendar for many years. Six to eight weeks in advance, we write in major blocks of various sorts of private time. We get these on the calendar before the events of church life begin to appear.

Second, we believe in taking the phone off the hook at various times in our home. Our telephone is "unringable" during dinnertimes, during moments of family discussion, and for periods when study or meditation is extremely necessary. In fifty years I can hardly ever recall a moment when being instantly accessible was a necessity. We have learned not to let the phone become our slave master.

Third, my wife and I learned several years ago that we needed to follow the discipline of marital quiet time. Our children have recognized our need for this, and they have refrained (as they have grown older) from unnecessary interruptions when Mom and Dad touch base with one another. Because my wife has centered the majority of her life in the home as wife and mother, I think marital quiet time is an absolute necessity, so I can share with her the things I have been doing out in the world, which she made possible by maintaining the home base.

Fourth, we have learned the law of quality time. When together as a family or as a couple, we are careful to be sharp and alert in our mental attitude, our dress, and our common courtesies. These are the things we would have done for church members; why not for our own intimate associates? It used to be my habit to fall apart on Monday mornings and come to the breakfast table unshaved, unwashed, and generally undressed. Gail pointed out that if I dressed for God and the congregation as I did on Sunday, what was I communicating to her by the way I dressed (or didn't dress) on Monday morning? I got the point.

Too many children and spouses see the Christian leader only after a day's work when he or she is exhausted and has nothing left to give. Gail and I have tried to schedule ourselves so that we give each other some of the very best times of the month when our minds, our emotions, and our bodies are alert and alive.

Fifth, we have learned to match our recreational pursuits with family needs. I realized early in my family life that I could not pursue a recreational life with friends and still have adequate amounts of time to pursue a second recreational life with my children. Therefore, I made choices to do things recreationally that my children could join me in doing: canoeing, camping, hiking, and other activities where our exercise and togetherness were able to be maximized. I fear too many fathers spend enormous amounts of energies on tennis courts, golf courses, and health clubs with other adults and then wonder why they

BUILDING BELOW THE WATERLINE

never have prime time with their children. I will admit, for the purposes of being transparent, that this has been an easy doctrine for me to embrace since I am a terrible tennis player, and I have never broken a hundred in golf (even for nine holes).

It is an age-old admonition: *Know thyself.* But just as significant is the proposal: *Know thy time.* By not knowing it, we are unable to budget it; like unbudgeted money, time therefore becomes hard to account for, and it is needlessly and tragically squandered. But by learning how to order the private time in our lives, we may increase the chances of being more alert, being more effective, and therefore being more the kind of people God wants us to be and our congregations need.

FOR FURTHER REFLECTION

1. How do you manage your time—or, more accurately, how do you manage yourself in time? How have you dealt with the explosion of technology (e.g., cell phones/smart phones, Facebook, Twitter) and the challenges it poses to ordering your private world?

2. Schedule a day alone. Whether you spend the day in nature or alone visiting a museum, use the day for silence and reflection.

3. Plan to have a morning of "Sabbath-time," either alone or with your spouse. Use the time to read, pray, write in your journal, and delight in God's presence. During this time, turn off your cell phone and computer.

KNEE-DRIVEN MINISTRY

*No time is so well spent every day
as that which we spend upon our knees.*

J. C. RYLE

I entered pastoral ministry in a time of great transition for the institutional church, the early sixties. In the eyes of many, the church had reached a low. "Relevance" was the buzzword, and the church, as well as preachers in general, were said to be irrelevant, perhaps even obsolete. As a result, a heavy percentage of my seminary classmates were headed for missions, para-church works, the chaplaincy, and a new discipline called counseling. Only a few of us really believed there could be a future in the pastorate.

My recollections are probably faulty, but as a new pastor, it seemed that every week someone from some new organization blew into town with a new program to sell me.

The opening pitch rarely varied: the church was dying, pastors were desperate, and here is a program (anointed by God) to save it all. Somewhere in the country (usually California) was a church that had adapted the program and was now growing by the "thousands" (count 'em).

I always found myself feeling guilty and a bit faithless as I would counter: "But that's in California," or "He's a different kind of leader," or "You don't know our people (or me)."

If it wasn't an organizational representative, it was one of my own people who had just returned from some church or conference saying, "You won't believe what God is doing there," or "You've got to attend their_____," or "You've got to start this_____."

I always tried to be nice in response, to show genuine interest and excitement, but sometimes it was difficult.

Only on Your Knees

Over the span of my pastoral years, I have seen a lot of trends, emphases, and calls to reengineer the church: church renewal, body life, personal evangelism, the charismatic gifts, Sunday school conventions, the Jesus movement, contemporary music (drums in the sanctuary?), church growth, the overhead projector and the "pastor-teacher," spiritual gift inventories, the pro-life movement, discipleship, concerts of prayer, cell groups, homeschooling, drama/dance, high liturgy, and country and western worship.

Some of them flared for a moment and then were gone; others have taken a solid position in our perspectives of ministry. But each, when it appeared, was just the latest in a series of solutions for the church's ills.

When I began public ministry, the slogan was "release the laity"; today, it's "be seeker-sensitive." Back then, we wanted to recover the "great hymnody of the church"; today, we seem to make them up as we go along. Yesterday, we talked about changing the world; today, it seems as if we'd just like to change ourselves. As they say about the weather, if you don't like what's here now, wait fifteen minutes.

As a much younger man, I found myself bewildered as I listened to all the claims. Thus, it was an important moment for me when I turned one day to an older, wiser man and said, "I find my head spinning trying to determine which of these approaches to lock on to. How do I choose? I can't do them all."

His answer has never left me: "Only on your knees will you and your leaders find the answer. There is a way for you and your church; but don't let anyone get between you and God as you seek out what it is." It was simple but absolutely profound. I have tried to follow that advice ever since.

Today, that advice is more important than ever. We abound with ministry strategies, techniques, resources, and talent I could never have imagined years ago. How wonderful! But how bewildering and potentially dangerous as well. It takes a perceptive person to find the substance.

More than a few young pastors (myself included) have gone to seminars that promised big stuff and come home with enthusiasm, expecting that something close to a reformation will break out in their town. A year later, some are in the process of leaving their ministries— heartbroken, rejected, and defeated. Casualties of the heart can be high.

Others, more fortunate, prepare to try something else. What worked in California, in Georgia, in Colorado (random examples), did not work in "my" community.

"Only on your knees," my friend said. The knees are the starting point. But from that starting point, I've discovered a cluster of "knee-driven" ministry principles that assist one in making good decisions about where to go and how to make strategic ministry choices. These principles are really gifts, something I didn't fully appreciate when I was a younger man. Only in retrospect do I see their value, and I have come to understand them as part of God's kindness, the way he responded when I went to my knees.

Value the Habitual Over the Novel

The first of these ministry principles came from my seminary professors. At the time I went to graduate school, my seminary was relatively young and struggling, barely surviving. Its professors had little more to offer than solid teaching and themselves as persons. They invested in young men and women, visiting in our homes (or hovels) when invited and asking us to theirs. In the context of their family lives and academic lives, they modeled stability, character, academic craftsmanship, and spiritual vitality. They let us know them.

Perhaps the greatest lesson was their insistence that I be faithful to the routines of life and ministry before I ever tried all of this "world-changing" stuff that is so seductive to the young, ambitious spirit. In other words, do the *right* things before you attempt the *big* things.

The routines (the right things) are the bread and butter of congregational life: being dependable, seeking excellence, caring for the hurting, being loyal to the biblical lifestyle, exalting Christ, developing people. They did it, those seminary professors, and the message was clear that we should do it too.

Learn Your History

Knowing the history of the Christian movement is a ballast to any ministry in periods of cultural turbulence and change (like now, for instance). History offers the fact that just about everything has been tried before in one way or another. History reveals both the possibilities and the potholes.

I invested much of my youthful energies in seeking to be an effective preacher, so I was tempted to compute my success in terms of how many people might be attracted to my preaching. In reading history, however, I learned that something more than preaching would validate the effectiveness of my ministry.

George Whitefield could easily have claimed a much larger number of responses to his preaching than John Wesley. But soon after both men were dead, it was clear that Wesley's work would impact future generations far more than Whitefield's. The reason? Wesley organized his followers into classes (a form of small groups); Whitefield never did. I came to understand that preaching without the reinforcement of deep community isn't really worth all that much.

Fly in Formation

Somewhere along the line, I learned to "fly in formation" with a select collection of authors. Paul Tournier taught me about people. Elton Trueblood gave me a love for ideas and the life of the mind. A.W. Tozer elevated my concept of God and worship. E. Stanley Jones became my inspiration for evangelism and the kingdom. John Stott taught me the power and dignity of preaching and gave me a hunger for biblical scholarship that had the "streets" of the real world in mind. And dear Henri Nouwen revealed to me the disciplines of the interior life. In these authors' books, I found a point of stability that protected me from running too quickly to the claims of instant success that came from other quarters.

As the years have passed, I have broadened the bandwidth of my reading and discovered that the God of all truth has salted creation with insights in all sorts of places. For example, Matthew Arnold's great ode to his father, a poem called "Rugby Chapel," is a great commentary on leadership:

If, in the paths of the world,
Stones might have wounded thy feet,
Toil or dejection have tried
Thy spirit, of that we saw
Nothing—to us thou wast still
Cheerful, and helpful, and firm!

In a time when leaders are tempted to "dumb down" their conduct and simply be like anyone else, Arnold's characterization of his father brings a lot of courage to me.

Godly Heroes

Like anyone else, I needed some godly heroes, and nineteenth-century Charles Simeon of Cambridge filled part of the bill. Serving for more than fifty years in an English parish, Simeon became my model pastor. More than a century ago, he understood (and practiced) leadership development, small group ministries, the theology of community, student evangelism, and church administration.

I have rarely faced a significant issue in ministry that Simeon did not face. And his experiences have saved me more than once from making a fool of myself.

Simeon's biographer, Hugh Evan Hopkins, is candid in describing his eccentricities: "There is no doubt that Charles Simeon was his own worst enemy when it came to establishing close friendships." At the time I read this, I was seriously questioning my own ability to be a good friend to others, and I caught this sentence and what followed with keen interest.

> *[Simeon's] angular and sometimes arrogant personality, against which he battled all this life long, more than anything else stood in the way. Though highly sensitive himself, it was a long time before he learned sensitivity to the feelings of others.*

I grew a lot from that simple insight.

In addition to heroes of the past, I have always had a man in my life whom I consider a mentor or spiritual father. Actually, there have been several. But the one who is most important lives two thousand miles away, and our contact is, at best, sporadic. However, when it occurs (by phone, letter, or personal visit), it is always intense and powerfully energizing.

This man whom I love (I shall leave his name mercifully anonymous lest he be deluged with calls) has always been there for me (and countless others). He has been there for my peak moments of ministry achievement and my deepest valleys of disappointment and humiliation. I have made few major decisions without his counsel.

My wife is also on this list. Gail is my opposite in temperament, and she has saved me from a thousand silly decisions with her sharp questions, her intuitive instincts, and her insistence on key life-loyalties. When I married her fifty years ago, a close friend admonished me, "She is God's gift to you. Don't squelch her giftedness—listen to her wisdom; honor her judgment." It was incredibly good advice. I fear that without it, I would have done the opposite.

Gifts of Friends and Foes

Then there has been the influence of friends. One category is a small group of men (in and out of the so-called ministry) who are simply good friends. These are comrades with whom I share experiences of life, who provide healthy perspective, prayer, laughter, and tears. I have not always had such friends, and it was in such times, when I'd isolated myself, that I had my greatest troubles and did stupid things.

The other category of friends is ministry-oriented. We have worked together, and our ongoing, day-to-day dialogue has been marked with candor and creativity. From them, I learned the value of the consultative ministry life.

An extension of this has been those boards with which a pastor works. No one ever taught me about the role of boards, and I fear that my earliest impression was that such groups were an obstacle course, more adversity than assistance. I changed that attitude, and in so doing, generally found that the boards to which I was accountable were quite able to help me discern and negotiate the changes and opportunities out there.

With a bit of reluctance, I find myself having to credit my critics with a lot of assistance over the years. To be frank, more than a few people simply have not liked me. Their varying observations of me run the gamut from shallow, "liberal," slick, arrogant, ambitious, or uncaring (and there are likely one or two who would include all of these on their lists). Some of them believe I should not be in ministry at all.

Had I blown off my critics and not listened to their voices, I would have missed the kernel of truth that lived in their harsh assessments. Had I ignored them, I would have probably fallen into the very traps they accused me of falling into. There are things I've not done, bandwagons I've not jumped on because of these people. And in most cases I'm glad. Although it has taken time, I've become grateful for them.

One of my critics, who later became a close friend, followed me out the door after one board meeting when I had allowed my feelings to show because I'd gotten a "no" in response to one of my "world-changing" ideas.

"You need to know," he said, "that your performance in there was not very classy. Moments like that will make this board increasingly reluctant to tell you what you need to hear, and that will ensure that you lose credibility with the congregation down the line."

How's that for a rebuke?

Grounded in Scripture

A love for the Bible has been an increasingly important ministry principle for me. You would think I would have figured this one out eons ago. I have virtually memorized Philippians 1, Ephesians 3, Acts 20, and 2 Corinthians 4. They have been the keel under my more visible life. Biblical personalities like Joseph, Isaiah, Ezra, Nehemiah, John the Baptist, and Paul have been my illuminators. They have taught me how to perservere, how to rebound from failure, how to handle defeat, and how to keep an eye on the mission God has given me.

One wonders if these heroes of the faith might roll their eyes if they saw all the brochures arriving on most pastors' desks, inviting them to some exotic place to acquire new ministry knowledge. Would they, in exasperation, say, "Oh, puh-leeze!" when they heard of one more book on leadership? Would they understand a person's ambivalence who says, "All this stuff is good, but somewhere along the line I've got to stay at home and do it."

As I look into the future and assess all the prognostications of the experts, I am once again bewildered by all that lies ahead. The futurists, the demographers, and the marketing people offer more information than I can adequately handle. I love reading it and talking about it. I even love, on those occasions when I'm invited, to contribute to it. But there is always the possibility of overload.

It doesn't seem much different today than it was all those years ago when I asked an older man how to sort through all those choices.

"Only on your knees," he said. And his advice to me then is just as good today.

FOR FURTHER REFLECTION

1. *How much time do you spend on your knees in prayer?*

2. *Who are your personal "godly heroes"? What special gifts have they given you through their lives and writings?*

3. *As you look at current ministry and leadership trends, which do you feel have substance, and which are not worth pursuing? Why or why not?*

PART TWO

THE OUTER LIFE

OF A LEADER

THE POWER OF
PUBLIC PRAYER

*The earnest prayer of a righteous person has
great power and produces wonderful results.*

JAMES 5:16 NLT

Years ago, I became friends with a man who had retired after many
years as a reporter and editor for a major newspaper. Over the years,
he told me stories from his journalistic career—many of them humor-
ous, others indescribably sad. My friend was a reluctant but frequent
observer of human cruelty, greed, exploitation, and immorality. When
I mentioned that fact to him, he did not disagree.

"After you've been in the news business for forty years," he said,
"you tend to develop a cynical and suspicious edge. You've heard every
kind of lie, you've seen every species of corruption, and you've been
witness to the sleaziest sorts of performances by folk the public thinks
are saints and heroes."

I asked him how he maintained his spiritual life amid such an environment: "Don't you feel sometimes as if you're living in a cesspool?
How do you avoid becoming polluted inside?"

"I'm not sure I've always kept spotless," he responded. "By the end of the week, I have often felt like a dirtied-up human being. That's why when I head into church on Sunday I need something to clean me up—a spiritual bath."

This friend did more than anyone else to confront me with what it means to pastor on a Sunday morning. I realized that his plight, while somewhat dramatic, was basically the same as that of most people who come to worship. Whether they know it or not, they also come out of a world saturated with evil. All of them need a bath. I began to wonder whether we provided it.

Garbage-Pail Prayers

Years after being alerted to this question, I preached at a worship service led by a friend, Bishop George McKinney of the Church of God in Christ. It was clear that he knew something about spiritual baths and the daily lives of worshipers.

Bishop McKinney appointed two elders to stand at the front of the sanctuary. One held a basket so worshipers could step forward and deposit written prayer requests. The other elder stood guard over a garbage pail. Into it worshipers were invited to pour their sins: either a written confession of attitudes and actions or the actual implements of evil from which they wanted to part. The pail often held syringes, pills, marijuana, stolen goods, and once, the bishop told me, a sawed-off shotgun.

Most of us are too subtle or cautious to adopt the bishop's methods. Perhaps we take too lightly the spiritual weight folk bring to the sanctuary on Sunday and, sadly, too often permit them to leave carrying the same baggage.

What to do with the "dirt" our people bring to church? As a preacher, my first instinct is to ask what my sermons might do for such a person. But one day it occurred to me that the "bath" is not necessarily in the preaching (although that is important), but probably during occasions I frequently neglected: the prayers.

It took me a while to realize the value of prayers offered during worship, perhaps because people were quick to comment on my sermon and only rarely mentioned the prayers. But as I got to know people deeply, I realized what they longed for (though sometimes were unable to express) was not so much for me to instruct them but to earnestly pray for them, to help lift their heavy burdens. They come each week wearied, muddied, and bloodied. Perhaps the most refreshing thing I can do for them is offer heartfelt prayer.

I realized I had never been taught, either formally or by example, how to pray effectively in worship. My public prayers all too often were little more than strings of religious phraseology. They were extemporaneous, but over time they developed a ritual quality of their own. Long-term attenders could almost predict what I would say. Painfully, I realized that few people were even listening to the prayers in a service; it was a time for minds to wander, drifting back to attention when they heard "and we ask this all in the name of him . . ."

How had I come to that conclusion? Dare I admit it was through my own experience? I had to muster all my concentration to listen to prayers myself. It was eerie to ponder the probability that on occasion, a thousand people might be present when a person was praying aloud, and that no one was involved in a word said.

Perhaps this is one reason that in nonliturgical congregations we see increased interest in scripted prayers. The ones supposedly spoken "from the heart" seem to have little thought (and therefore content) behind the heart. Even my friends in liturgical churches, however, admit that well-crafted prayers don't keep them or their congregations from sometimes approaching public prayer in a perfunctory manner.

That's why I decided to ask some hard questions about the meaning and placement of the various prayers in a worship service. I wanted to be sure that each time we addressed almighty God, we did so with the proper intent and content.

In worship, I discovered, there are at least six kinds of prayer to be offered on the congregation's behalf. The unknowing leader may confuse the six, mix their purposes, and diffuse the effectiveness of that "bath" my friend came to worship to receive.

The Invocation

The first prayer of worship, usually called the invocation, has only one purpose: to invite and then acknowledge the presence of God among the assembled worshipers. To invoke is to request God's openness to the words and thoughts of the people. It's a prayer to set aside this as a special time, a hallowed time unlike any other during the week. Holy activity is about to commence: worship, humankind's most important event.

The invocation is not a prayer for people or the issues of the present age, nor a rehearsal of the theological knowledge of the one praying. Rather, it is a humble acknowledgment that those gathered are looking heavenward with thanksgiving, asking God's presence in what is about to be said and done.

My friends in liturgical churches say all of this in the concise "In the name of the Father, the Son, and the Holy Spirit, Amen." While I may use a few more words, our invocations focus on the same thing:

We invite your presence, our Father, through the kindness of Jesus Christ. Having finished a week of work, of study, of play, we're here to worship, guided by the Holy Spirit. We have joined together to express our appreciation for the ways you have safely and lovingly led us . . .

The Pastor's Prayer

Another prayer of the worship service, perhaps the most cleansing of all, is often called the pastor's prayer. In my pastorates, it became the one prayer of worship I steadfastly refused to delegate as long as I was in the service.

I deem the pastor's prayer on a par with the pastor's sermon. If the sermon is the pastor's opportunity to hold up the Word of God to the people, the pastor's prayer is the opportunity to hold up the people to God. It is not unlike those occasions when Moses interceded for the people of Israel. And it is the congregation's opportunity (and, I believe, privilege) to hear their pastor pray for them.

As a pastor, I often invited my congregation to join me to kneel for this prayer. I made kneeling an option, recognizing that some would have physical difficulty kneeling in a church without kneelers. I knelt on one knee myself and led the congregation from that position.

Kneeling or standing, I found it important to pray this prayer away from the pulpit. Usually I knelt at the head of the center aisle. That proximity to the people provided a point of contact for us all. It made my sense of praying more real, and I suspect the people felt more keenly that I was one of them.

The pastor's prayer usually has four parts. In traditional liturgies, some of these parts may be separated into prayers of their own.

Acknowledging God

The first is an acknowledgment of God himself and his involvement in our personal and congregational life. We need to be reminded who God is—his attributes and actions. It is a time to reaffirm the majesty of God, to be reminded of the smallness of our world in contrast to his infinite dwelling place.

All week long, our world appears larger and larger as it seeks to intimidate, dominate, and exploit. It would be easy for my journalist friend to arrive at worship with the unspoken notion that reality is rotten and undependable. He, like others, needs to be reminded of another reality, that God is not sullied by the machinations of a sinful race.

Thus, a pastor's prayer needs to center on at least one aspect of God and our response to him. Majesty, holiness, kindness, and power are merely a few examples.

> *Lord, in a world dishing out more than ample amounts of harshness, your kindness is a special reality to us. You treat us not according to what we deserve, but according to what we need. You give us gifts and capacities to enjoy the world you created; you give us abilities to love and receive love, to be able to forgive and forget. And most of all, you give us your Son, Jesus Christ. You are a kind God, our Father, and we love you.*

Confession and Forgiveness

In contrast to such an affirmation, the second part of the pastor's prayer is usually the clear confession that we are sinners, that our past week was marked with attitudes and actions that grieve our heavenly Father. This confession concludes with an affirmation of God's forgiveness for all who are humble and contrite in spirit.

It is no accident that Isaiah felt an immediate urge to confess his sinfulness the minute he visualized the glory of God in the temple (Isa. 6). There is an unbreakable link between the two experiences. We help people by offering opportunity to face frankly one's sin and resolve the matter with God.

This is a special and most poignant part of worship. As pastor, I speak to God on behalf of my friend the reporter, leading him and others into God's presence with a realization that we are contaminated with the sin of this world. Together we need cleansing; we need to know we are once again clean. For me this moment is both tender and exhilarating.

In Bishop McKinney's church, the choir sang a lively soul song after people had had a chance for repentance and forgiveness: "Jesus heard my prayer, and everything's okay."

This part of the pastor's prayer is not something to pass by lightly. It admits our bent toward rebellion and the importance of the cross in realigning the believer with the Father. Regarded properly, this can be a moment of liberation, of straightened accounts, for many who have come in desperate guilt and shame for failures in previous hours.

Who of us here, Father, would not quickly admit we have disappointed you on many occasions this past week? The thoughts and attitudes we have often nurtured are things for which we are truly sorry. We repent of them. Some of us could quickly admit to deeds done or not done of which we are frankly ashamed. Some of us have come here today, Lord, bearing resentments and jealousies that would be terribly embarrassing if others knew about them. We confess these, Father. We need liberation from our sins. Thank you for hearing our personal confessions.

Prayer for Our World

The third aspect of the pastor's prayer looks outward upon our world of revolution, starvation, disasters, elections, and achievements—the macro events people hear about throughout their week. Somehow, my prayer must put these things into an eternal perspective and model how to pray in light of such events. All of us need to be reminded regularly that each world event concerns the Father and therefore must concern his children. Not to pray for these matters is to imply by silence that what happens in the sanctuary has no relevance to affairs during the other six days of the week. As a pastor, I found it important to make sure that on the way to church each Sunday morning I heard the latest news broadcast to be sure my prayer agenda was up to date.

A part of our world hurts today, Lord. Men and women who think and feel just like us have no homes, no food, nothing to provide for their children's welfare. Father, many grieve today over the loss of loved ones in a tragic accident. Presidents and prime ministers engage one another today, Lord; they desperately need wisdom . . .

The Needs of the People

The final part of the pastor's prayer centers on the needs of the people themselves. I have rarely come to this point of the prayer without remembering the story Henri Nouwen tells about the abbot of a Trappist monastery who met his monks as they returned from the fields each evening, dirtied and wearied. As they approached, he would raise both arms to receive them and cry out, "Are any of you in trouble?" It was a time for each monk to pause, reflect upon anything amiss within the heart or among relationships, and find relief in God's promised kindness and grace.

The pastor's prayer, therefore, is a prayer for those who are in trouble and know it—for the worker who fears the loss of a job, for the person facing a doctor's appointment and potentially bad news, for parents raising children who do not seem to like them, for the single woman who is desperately lonely, for the teenager worrying about his sexuality. Mentioning such needs each week helps people in the pews sense that their individual needs are being offered up, even if not specifically mentioned. Here, we hold up our arms for those in trouble. If we speak in tenderness, in hope, in authenticity (meaning *real* words describing *real* situations), and with urgency, the people will know they have been spiritually bathed.

> *Father, some of us came here in deep pain: the pain of the body, the pain of wounded relationships, the pain of pure, unrelenting fear. Father, some of us badly need help and encouragement . . .*

Wise pastors also intercede for various ministries in the congregation, not all of them at once, of course, but perhaps one each week.

The pastor's prayer can often be concluded with a song by the congregation. Some of my most memorable occasions were when we sang the Lord's Prayer without instruments. The sense of being welded together before the throne of God lingered with me for many days afterward.

In smaller congregations, parts of the pastor's prayer can be shared with the congregation in what is sometimes called "conversational prayer." When our sanctuary was smaller, I occasionally invited worshipers to stand and read one (I carefully held them to just one) verse of Scripture that exalted the living God. What often happened was a beautiful mosaic of verses that directed our thoughts to many aspects of God's being and purposes.

Equally memorable were invitations to the congregation to stand and speak one sentence of praise to the Lord. I found it important to give specific instructions ahead of time in order to fend off the one or two folks who might dominate the occasion. On the other hand, those not used to public prayer were encouraged to participate, since the requirement was only one sentence.

The Dedication of Gifts

A third prayer of the worship service usually comes before or after the offering. Recently, I sat in a congregation where the offering was received by ushers, an equal number of men and women. Afterward, the ushers walked to the front and held the plates high above their heads to offer them to the Father. We sang the doxology and then were led in prayer by one who understood that the money in the plates symbolized our week's labor. It was a touching moment.

What was this prayer doing? It was applying meaning and value to our work. We were saying, "We offer you, Father, the firstfruits of our work." The pastor who prayed used words that let us know he was aware that we had worked hard, that the dollars in the plate had not come easily, that to give them was an act of cheerful obedience. I was impressed that the pastor who dedicated our gifts took them seriously, not as income for the church budget or benevolence program but as the fruits of our work.

> *Some of us who are here today, our Father, are tired and bruised because we have had a hard week of work. But we have done our best at jobs that are sometimes exciting, sometimes boring. We have joyfully brought the evidence of our labor, and we present to you today a portion of what you have made possible for us to earn.*

The Prayer of Illumination and Submission

Scripture is not fully appreciated without the illuminating work of the Holy Spirit searching the heart, applying truth, and bringing people to conviction. Thus, another possible prayer in the worship service is the prayer of submission to the Word of God.

In some liturgical services, it is common for the congregation to sing a hymn before the sermon. During the singing, the preacher kneels and prays for himself. As he consecrates himself to the work of the Spirit, the congregation becomes aware that the preacher works under divine accountability and that what they are about to hear is God's living Word for them.

This same preacher may call the congregation to prayerful attention as he opens the Scriptures. In this brief moment, all are commended to the work of the Holy Spirit and are challenged to listen in submission to the Scriptures.

The time has come for us to open the Scriptures, Lord, to listen to your voice as it comes to us through the inspiring work of the Holy Spirit. Give us an ability to hear what is important and to place it into our experiences. We submit to your insight and guidance . . .

The Prayer of Decision

Assuming that a sermon connects God's Word to a worshiper's life, it is appropriate for the worship leader to end a sermon with a reflective prayer, one that calls the listener to a point of closure. This prayer should not be a review of the sermon's major points but a petition that God's Word might be clear to each worshiper and properly applied to his or her life.

All of us—beginning with myself—are startled with the richness of these truths, Father. They call us to something higher and more powerful than we've ever known. We need to do something about what you've said to us today. Help us to discover what that could be . . .

The Benediction

Sometimes called the *ascription*, the benediction is the concluding prayer in most worship services. All too often, it is merely a signal that a service is almost over; people use the time to put away hymn books, grab their coats, or even get a head start to the parking lot.

We are not merely closing a service with prayer. Rather, we are offering a final affirmation of blessing upon our people and thanksgiving to God for having been present.

The prayer should be brief. There is no need to rehearse the events of the morning; this is a simple acknowledgement of God's faithfulness and a pronouncement of his blessing, as the traditional biblical benedictions do. Few things are more moving than for a pastor to raise his hands in blessing over the people and pray them Godspeed in their journeys. It is the final word to the children of God as they reenter the world. It should be encouraging, tender, and affirming, reminding them that they go with the covering hand of the Father and Shepherd.

> *Father, we ask your blessing as we leave this place. We have done our best to tell you that we love you, that we're grateful for your kindnesses, that we want to know more of you. We return to our homes and places of work with confidence in your promised care and guidance. Our expectation is that you will help us seize the hours before us to advance the work of your kingdom.*

What my friend the journalist means when he says he needs a spiritual bath is that he is in need of someone who knows how to pray for him, especially when he doesn't feel he can pray for himself. In the corporate prayers during worship, ministers have an opportunity to provide that sense of cleansing. But it takes time to plan, to think through one's prayers, and to make sure that each one contains what both the congregation and God ought to hear from the minister, the intercessor. Perhaps then my journalist friend can return to the newspaper business on Monday ready to take on life in that world with a bit of kingdom power.

> *Holy Father, may those of us who are pastors and spiritual directors come to increasing appreciation of the rich privilege of holding the people up to you. Give us the insight that helps us understand their needs. Give us the faith that causes us to be confident in the power of intercession. Give us a vision of yourself and your majesty, and our-*

selves and our brokenness, that causes our prayers for the people to have reality and power, we ask in the name of Jesus. Amen.

FOR FURTHER REFLECTION

1. How would you describe the quality of public prayers in your congregation? The responsiveness of the hearers?

2. Pick one or two of the types of prayers mentioned and try composing a prayer in your own words that you can share with your congregation.

3. During your Sunday worship and throughout the week, how often do you pray specifically for the needs of those you lead?

THE 3:00 A.M. PHONE CALL

Then I will give you shepherds after my own heart, who
will lead you with knowledge and understanding.

JEREMIAH 3:15

Remember that political ad in which the White House phone rings
at 3 A.M. and someone has to answer? I know the experience. Sort of.

My phone call came late one afternoon. The caller, a church attendee
I knew only casually, said he was at the hospital where his wife, Josie, was
dying of cancer and might not last the night. Could I come right away?

Even though this call came many years ago, I'm still embarrassed
when I remember that my first thought was something like: *Where is*
our pastoral care staff person? I don't do hospitals. I'm the one who preaches,
who leads, who casts vision. Oh, and I'm the one always telling people
(from the pulpit) that I love them and care for them.

The caller said his dying wife was terrified. Despite the sedatives she
had been given, she was almost violent and could hardly be restrained.
"Perhaps you can say something to her that will help her to relax and go
to sleep," he said.

The hospital was a twenty-minute drive. When I arrived, a family friend met me and escorted me to the room. On the way, she described how Josie was thrashing about in fear. Occasionally she would scream. No one, the friend said, knew what to do. Even the doctors and nurses seemed stymied.

I took a deep breath and entered the room. There were maybe eight people around the bed: a doctor or two, the nurses, Josie's husband, and a daughter. Then I saw Josie in the bed.

"Josie!" I said as I approached. I said her name firmly, as if to establish my presence with some authority.

"Pastor Mac!" she responded. The circle broke as everyone stepped back to make room for me.

Frankly, I wasn't sure what was appropriate for the moment. It's awkward when even the physicians relinquish their space at the bedside to me. All I can remember is that something inside of me said, "Take charge; be a pastor!"

"Josie," I said, "this is a terrible moment for you, isn't it? You must be very frightened."

"Yes, Pastor Mac," Josie replied, her eyes darting toward her husband and her daughter. "I don't know what to do. I can't leave them. I have to get better." Then she repeated, "I don't know what to do."

What she really wanted to do was sit up and get out of that bed. I sensed she was about to become agitated again, so I put my hands on her emaciated shoulders and, as gently as I could, pressed her back into the pillow. I remember the powerful silence in the room as everyone else looked on. No one objected to what I'd done so far. Perhaps they thought I knew exactly what I was doing.

An idea came to me. I leaned closer so my face dominated Josie's line of sight, and said: "Josie, listen to me. Look into my eyes. I have a thought for you."

"Yes, Pastor Mac?"

"I want you to listen to some words from God. Just listen! Okay?"

"Okay."

I began, "The Lord is my shepherd; I have everything that I need." I recited Psalm 23 slowly, deliberately, carefully pronouncing each word. Then, "Did you hear me, Josie? 'I'—that's you, Josie—'have . . . everything . . . that . . . I . . . need.'"

"Yes, Pastor Mac, I heard you." She repeated, "I have everything that I need."

I went on. "God makes me lie down in green pastures. God leads me beside cool waters. God restores my soul."

I simplified the psalm a bit and repeated the words. "God . . . makes . . . me . . . lie . . . down . . . God gives me cool water . . . God brings strength to my heart. . . . Did you hear that, Josie?"

"I heard it, Pastor Mac." She was looking straight into my eyes and hanging on every word. Sensing a bit of relaxation in her shoulders, I went on with the psalm, speaking of the pathways of righteousness, the dangerous valleys where God is present, the shepherd's rod and staff, the tables of food, and the oil that heals and protects. Finally, I reached the last lines and expanded them a bit: "And I shall dwell in the house of the Lord for ever . . . and ever . . . and ever."

As distinctly as I could, I said, "Josie, you're in those words. They're about you. You are one who is in God's care. You've been a wonderful wife and mother. You've been a good friend. And now it may be time to go and live in God's house for ever and ever and ever. Someday we're going to join you. Each of us." I named Josie's husband and their daughter. "They're going to be there with you."

"Are you sure?" she asked.

"I'm sure," I said. "And I want you to know that everyone here loves you and is thankful to you. I want you to rest now and let God take you where he wants to lead you. Josie, don't be afraid."

"Are you sure it's okay to go, Pastor Mac?"

"Yes, I'm sure, Josie."

Then Josie did something I'll never forget. She looked away from me and spoke to her husband: "Thank you for being such a good husband to me." And to her daughter: "I love you; I'm so proud to be your mother." And then to the medical people: "Thank you for taking such good care of me." After a few words to each friend in the circle, she thanked me. Then Josie closed her eyes, sank into a calm sleep, and, about an hour later, left our presence.

A Ministry of Divine Connection

I have been a pastor for over fifty years. When I try to characterize the nature of my work, that story seems to sum up the core task of a pastor. Call it a priestly function or a pastoral one, it's all the same: helping people connect with God.

A desperate husband needed someone to bring spiritual strength into one of the worst moments of his life. Medical personnel who had exhausted their means needed someone who could speak into a patient's heart. A fearful and confused woman needed someone who could offer her a word of guidance from God. On that day, I was given the grace to be the person who did all of this.

The psalm that I spoke into Josie's heart has been familiar to me since age five, when I first memorized it because my grandmother bribed me with a dollar bill—big money in those days—to quote it without error. It took less than an hour to do the job.

As an adult, Psalm 23 served as something of a tranquilizer when I was troubled and couldn't sleep. Over and over, I would quote it to myself until the sensation of following Jesus the Shepherd on secure paths toward green pastures and cool waters overcame my inner turbulence.

The psalm served me in another way, many years into my ministry, when I began to weary of church leadership. My job had changed as our congregation grew, and it changed me from a pastor who knew something about almost everyone in the church to a CEO. Formerly, I had engaged with people; now I ran an organization. I felt guilty that I could no longer say as Jesus did, "I am the good shepherd; I know my sheep and my sheep know me." Truth be told, I didn't know most of them, and they didn't know me.

Quoting Psalm 23 to myself one day, I was struck with the notion that the psalm was really a job description for a shepherd or a pastor. Why had I not seen this before?

Traditional scholarship attributes this psalm to David, who knew sheep and shepherding intimately. Another psalmist, musing upon David's journey wrote, "[God] chose David his servant and took him from the sheep pens; from tending the sheep he brought him to be the shepherd of his people . . . and David shepherded them with integrity of heart" (Ps. 78:70–72).

During his apprentice years in the field, how many times had David picked up on the fear of his flock when they sensed danger? How many times had he found it necessary to lead them through dangerous valleys and on to greener pastures and cooler waters? How often had he used oil to clean the sheep's wounds or protect them from the annoyance of insects? How often had he rescued a helpless lamb from a precarious situation?

It's no wonder that when David later attempted to describe the nature of God, he used a word picture with which he was thoroughly familiar. *God is like a shepherd.* Implication? If you are a part of God's flock, you have everything you need.

A Dirty Job

In modern times, we tend to glamorize shepherds. We picture them in clean clothes carrying cute little lambs on their shoulders. Be careful!

The fact is that ancient shepherds (I can't speak for them today) were generally found on the bottom rung of society. Rarely did they own the sheep they tended. Rather, they were like "temps" who minded sheep in the countryside on behalf of sheep-owners who probably lived nearby. Let's be frank: most shepherds in Bible times were not esteemed.

When Moses fled Egypt, the only job he could get was as a shepherd. For forty years, he tended the flock of his father-in-law, Jethro. The subtle biblical message: Look how far Moses fell, from an Egyptian palace to tending sheep. It raises the question: What does shepherding do to a man? Moses, David, and others did their graduate work in leadership in the shepherding business.

It's interesting that angels selected shepherds as the audience for their Christmas recital in the skies near Bethlehem. Shepherds are credited as the first worshipers at the manger scene. Why?

Later, Jesus would liken himself to a shepherd. Why not a military general, or a business owner, or a high priest in Jerusalem? Clearly, he was more drawn to the notion of sheep that trusted their shepherd and followed obediently.

Jesus told the story of the shepherd who, at the risk of his own life, went into the wilderness to search for one lost sheep. Was this really good business? Or was it an exaggerated story to make the point that one sheep (or person) was equivalent in value to the ninety-nine others who remained with the flock?

Paul would suggest that the Ephesian church leaders draw their understanding of church leadership from a shepherd. "Keep watch over yourselves and all the flock . . . be shepherds of the church of God . . . wolves will come in among you and will not spare the flock" (Acts 20:28–29).

In keeping with the notion that most shepherds are not sheep-owners but sheep-tenders, Paul reminded the Ephesian leaders that their "flock" was really God's, and that they were the go-to guys to guarantee the church's integrity.

Back to Psalm 23. If this is something of a job description for pastoral leadership, there is some thinking to do.

A Pastoral Job Description

The psalm, first of all, suggests that a shepherd—not unlike a mother—makes sure that sheep have everything they need in order to stay healthy: water, grass, and a safe place to rest. These are typical concerns of a nurturer, one responsible for the sheep's well-being.

Then the psalm offers another view of leadership. The same shepherd who provides grass and water leads the flock along pathways that can be challenging, even threatening, and valleys where predators lurk intent on taking down a lamb or two. This shepherd knows how to keep his sheep calm and keep the wolves away. This is quite some shepherd. *This,* David seems to be saying, *is who God is to me.*

The word *pastor* is built on the notion of that kind of shepherd. It's associated with the feeding of sheep as well as the spiritual feeding of people. In fact, it offers a fresh view of Jeremiah 3:15—"I will give you shepherds after my own heart, who will lead you with knowledge and understanding."

In the New Testament, the word for *shepherd* and *pastor* became the same. Want to pastor a church? Then you're a shepherd (in the likeness of God), and the people you lead are your sheep.

I would contend that the pastor/shepherd is the core element of any group that hints at being a congregation. The clearest description of a church can be found in Jesus' words, ". . . where two or three gather together because they are mine" (Matt. 18:20 NLT). My contention would be that within that "two or three" there will always be someone that Jesus "gifts" with the pastoral role. Who is he or she? What do they do?

Such a person—like a shepherd—has a simple job: to gather the people; to see that they are refreshed spiritually and prepared for dangerous pathways. Most of this they do by simply being there—by monitoring the soul.

Know Your Flock

Years ago, Harry Emerson Fosdick wrote:

I distrust a preacher to whom sermons seem the crux of his functioning. The temptations of a popular preacher—if he is only that—are devastating. He is applauded by fans, credited with a Christian selflessness he cannot claim, and enticed by many listeners to think of himself more highly than he ought to think. . . . Let any preacher who has such an experience humbly run home and pray to be delivered from its seductions. Only the grace of God can deliver him—that and a genuine care for persons, so that to him, as to Jesus, all that matters in a crowd is the opportunity to get vitally in touch with some individual.

It would be interesting to ask someone who knows these sorts of things, "What is the maximum size of a flock that one shepherd can lead? When does a flock get so large that one shepherd is no longer able to lead, feed, and protect them?"

When I started in ministry, the majority of pastors led flocks of ninety to three hundred people. Most pastors had no assistants, answered their own telephones, and were reasonably available to anyone in and beyond their church. Their job was quite similar to that of a shepherd.

As a child, I would often hear my father (a pastor) say to my mother as he left our home, "I'll be calling until supper time." That was 80 percent of his job: calling. In homes, at businesses, whenever people were in the hospital. A call consisted of Bible reading, prayer, probing questions about personal faith, and a challenge. Pastors knew their people, and the people knew their pastor. Like shepherds and sheep.

By the way, I am not pining for those days, believe me. Let's not get too romantic here. Those times were often times of low salaries, parsonages or manses, and 24/7 expectations by the flock.

On the other hand, is the present situation in most congregations any improvement? What are we saying when the most direct connection people have with their pastor is listening to a sermon? Is there any kind of personal engagement with the people who make up the flock?

I often recall the woman in my church who was easy for all of us to ignore. She was chronically depressed and usually medicated. One day, I saw her from a distance and shouted out instinctively, "Hello, Marilyn. How are you?" Then I turned to other things. But she stood next to me and said, "Pastor Mac, you say, 'Hello, Marilyn. How are you?' But you don't really want to know. You don't have time to find out."

She was right. She said what a lot of others probably wanted to say but lacked the "courage" that medication sometimes offers. Marilyn's words continue to haunt me.

I no longer believe the biblical title of pastor applies if it takes three weeks for someone to get an appointment. I do not believe the biblical word for pastor applies when someone can say, "I've heard him (or her) preach for three years, but we've never met."

I am not criticizing megachurch leaders. I know and respect many of them. I've been one. To be honest, I loved most (not all) of my job when I led a larger congregation. But I suspect we would be more honest if we referred to a megachurch leader as a bishop or—call it what it is—a CEO or a president. But—and here's my point—let's save the title of pastor for the man or woman who goes face to face with people, whatever their need. Like in that hospital room.

The pastor does not "shepherd" people by merely preaching to them. Pastoring works through personal relationship, through personal prayer, through personal instruction. It responds to questions, confronts when there is sin, and confirms when God is speaking. A pastor's whole life becomes a model for people to follow.

This was Paul's idea when he wrote to Timothy, "Set an example for the believers in speech, in life, in love, in faith, and in purity" (1 Tim. 4:12). Or later when he wrote, "Be diligent in these matters; give yourself wholly to them, so that everyone may see your progress" (v. 15).

We must be careful not to think that we have pastored through books, DVDs, websites, and sermons. Pastoring—shepherd style—is up close and personal. It demands a willingness to answer the phone.

Many years after that hospital visit with Josie, I invited a surgeon to speak to a seminary class I was teaching. Among other things, he said, "When we doctors enter a hospital room, we bring a word about physical possibilities, but when you pastors enter that room, you bring a word of hope, a word from God."

He described perfectly what I had tried to do that day. And that's what answering the phone can lead to.

FOR FURTHER REFLECTION

1. *In your experience, have you known pastors whom you consider to be true shepherds? What kind of an impact have they had upon your life?*

2. *Think about times when you've been expected to offer words of comfort to someone. How did you feel in this situation, and what did you say?*

3. *What are the challenges of pastoring a large congregation? What are the challenges of pastoring a small one? How can the leader of any size congregation develop true personal connections with his or her "flock"?*

WHEN THINGS GET UGLY

*Alas! Much has been done of late to promote the
production of dwarfish Christians. Poor, sickly believers
turn the church into a hospital, rather than an army.
Oh, to have a church built up with the deep godliness
of people who know the Lord in their very hearts, and
will seek to follow the Lamb wherever he goes!*

CHARLES SPURGEON

My first crack at shepherding a congregation came during semi-nary days when a group of twenty families, ranchers and farmers liv-ing on the Kansas-Colorado border, offered a parsonage and a small paycheck if I would be their pulpit guy. Gail and I enthusiastically en-tered the rural culture to serve the people. They taught us much, and we loved them in return.

A few months into this experience, the deacons convened a meet-ing to resolve a business issue. I can't remember the subject matter, but I do recall that people I really cared for began to say things to each other that left Gail and me devastated. It was like being parents of children fighting in the backseat. It sounds prideful, but we couldn't believe that people under our ministry influence could act so unpleasantly.

After the meeting, a woman approached Gail and me to say, "Now you know who we really are. And some day you'll be just like us."

Gail responded, "No! We'll never allow ourselves to become like that." A bold assertion, of course; but we were young and self-confident.

Several times in my years of ministry, I have seen repeat performances of that evening. And each time, I have struggled with the same disappointment.

My go-to Bible story in such moments is Moses, coming down from Mount Sinai to find the children of Israel *(brats* might be a better word) dancing around a golden calf with his brother Aaron's fingerprints all over it.

On the mountaintop, Moses had been as close to God as you can get, and now he reentered a world below (which is the "real world"?) where people couldn't sustain even a few days of faithfulness on their own.

We have to admit that, in the process of leadership, there are moments of extreme disappointment and disillusionment when people we lead utterly fail to live up to our expectations. Most of my own writings have been upon the failures of leaders (and especially my own). But there is a time to ask: *What does the leader do when the people fail?*

On such occasions, it is wise for the leader to begin by contemplating how earlier leaders coped. I am not speaking of their organizational, problem-solving methods. I'm talking about how they resolved the anger, discouragement, or blaming spirit that threatened to overwhelm their own souls. That's how Moses became my main man for low-end times.

Leading a Repulsive Bunch

When you read the stories of Moses and Israel, you have to marvel at the defiant, complaining, unappreciative ways of the Hebrews and ask yourself why (or how) Moses ever stuck with them.

Knowing myself, I would have been tempted to resign and send my resume to the Amorites, Jebusites, or other local "-ites." Anyone else need a liberator?

What I never appreciated until recently was the significance of Israel being a community of ex-slaves with all the attitudes and default behaviors that resulted from four hundred years of oppression. As many years as I have known their story, it never occurred to me that when one generation after another has been denied essential human rights and lost its dignity, such people will become seriously impaired in their ability to make decisions, be loyal, trust leaders, hope for tomorrow, or even get along with each other.

I used to wonder why Israel never gave Moses suitable recognition for his leadership. No banquet, no new car, no trip to the Holy Land (just kidding).

When did Moses fully realize what kind of people he had on his hands? Was it when, at age forty, he intervened on behalf of a Hebrew and discovered no one was appreciative? Was it when Pharaoh implemented the bricks-without-straw policy and the people blamed Moses, saying, "You've made us a stench to Pharaoh"? Was it when they complained about bitter water? If we seek to pry into Moses' heart, there is little to go on. Most of the time, he appears to have handled things rather admirably, I think.

Leaders today may want to think about what characterizes people who enter the Christian community from lives of raw unbelief. That's what we have to look forward to in coming years. Ours is no longer a

Christianized society where most people come to us with a basic understanding of biblical ways and norms. The restraints and disciplines of a strong community life no longer apply.

The result: newcomers to church life arrive with a host of behaviors and attitudes not unlike Israel. They like Jesus a lot, but sports, shopping, fun, and moneymaking are also pretty attractive.

Shallow Spirituality

I think the day Moses saw the golden calf was when he *really* wondered if there was a future.

Moses had been on the mountaintop for an extended time with God. Down below, the people apparently succumbed to their abandonment issues, and they convinced Aaron to aid them in constructing a more visible "god" to worship. "As for this fellow Moses who brought us up out of Egypt, we don't know what has happened to him" (Exod. 32:1). How quickly some leaders can be forgotten!

An image made of gold, which Aaron would dismiss later, saying it simply popped out of the fire, was deliberately fashioned with tools. Almost immediately, the Israelites began to regard the idol as the "god" who brought them out of Egypt. Then an orgy of pagan ritual began. It appears to have taken just a few days for all of this to happen.

Do you need an illustration of shallow spirituality? You've got it right here. And shallow spirituality is what Moses saw when, accompanied by Joshua, he came down from the mountain. The two saw what was going on and couldn't believe their eyes.

Curiously, God had warned Moses that something like this was in motion, but he had to see it for himself. God had said, "They are a stiff-necked people" (Exod. 32:9). On the mountain, it appears that Moses had to intervene lest an impatient God impose a harsh brand of justice.

But now that he saw what was going on, it was Moses' turn to go ballistic. He smashed the stone tablets he'd brought down from the mountain. He pummeled the golden idol into powder, mixed it with water, and made the Israelites drink it. Some angry man, that Moses. Ever been tempted to emulate him?

As the story ends, we find Moses interceding for the people (has he cooled off by now?), and God striking the people with the judgment of a plague "because of what they did with the calf Aaron had made" (v. 35).

The story reminds me of how bad things can get in some leadership situations. Others may say, "My story is worse than that!" Me? I've known a few moments when I felt people imploded spiritually, but I've never been close to what Moses experienced. Nevertheless, I identify with his bewilderment, fury, and sense of devastation. Most leaders can feel it.

Fleeing the "Über-Temptation"

The scholars I've read find it difficult to put the stories in this section of Exodus in perfect sequence. But I find it significant that what we read next is about the tent Moses pitched, known as the "tent of meeting" (the same tent mentioned in the Extreme Faith chapter).

This tent, the writer says, was located "outside the community some distance away." Its purpose: to be a place where people could go "to inquire of the Lord." Exodus 33:7 suggests that anyone could approach the tent, but we only hear of Moses doing so.

Why does the writer place the story of the tent right after the golden calf incident? Perhaps the writer is saying, "This is how Moses maintained his equilibrium in stressful moments." When everything fell apart, when even his brother, Aaron, momentarily betrayed the cause, Moses had a place to go where he could reinforce himself in the presence of God.

That raises a question for me: Do most leaders have something similar to Moses' tent? Let me suggest that an office, from which most leaders operate, won't do. It's simply too distracting a place.

One of the über-temptations of a leader is to become so absorbed in the fortunes of his organization or church that his perception of reality becomes controlled by what people are or are not doing. A leader is on quicksand when the applause or the apathy of followers becomes the measure of his success and satisfaction.

For Moses, when things turned ugly, he regularly headed to the tent for a reality check. It appears to have been a quiet place, separated from business and politics, where God could be heard at whisper level. When Moses started for the tent, all of Israel seemed to be aware. Each person, the text says, stood and privately worshiped when Moses went there.

That description of Moses walking to the tent and the people standing at worshipful attention recalls for me a boyhood memory of my father, then a pastor, who would walk down the aisle of the sanctuary on Sunday morning after the people had gathered.

At the front, he would kneel near the pulpit and silently pray. All of us were treated to the sight of a pastor praying for his congregation on his knees. That weekly sight made a lifelong impression on me. I wonder how many congregations ever see their leader pray, *really intercede,* for them?

In the same way, I see Moses headed toward the tent in times of trouble. In this case, the people have failed. Does he worry that there may be no tomorrow? Has this golden calf incident imperiled the dream of becoming God's people? Who knows what swirled in his head.

Exodus 33 provides a powerful description of the kinds of conversation Moses and God had in the tent. Again, I concede that it is conjecture, but these accounts (the golden calf story and the tent conversation) seem to be adjacent to each other for some purpose, and I believe it is to show us what was most on Moses' mind as he dealt with the hurt and the anger of what Israel had just done.

In Tents and Purposes

What is Moses seeking as he enters the tent? Assurance that God is not going to give up on them? Reaffirmation of God's promises? I suspect that he feels unbelievably weak, and he needs to know where the energy to keep going will come from. That's what I would be looking for.

What do leaders pray for when they go to their own versions of the tent? What themes stabilize a downhearted leader in the fog of spiritual warfare?

A mid-twentieth-century preacher on revival, Leonard Ravenhill, wrote in a rather poetic fashion:

> *Poverty-stricken as the church is today in many things, she is most stricken here, in the place of prayer. We have many organizers, but few agonizers; many players and payers, few pray-ers; many singers, few clingers; lots of pastors, few wrestlers; many fears, few tears; much fashion, little passion; many interferers, few intercessors; many writers, but few fighters. Failing here, we fail everywhere.*

We get an idea of how Moses talked with God if we muse on the issues he raises once he is inside the tent. These are noted in Exodus 33.

Presence

On Moses' agenda is something about holy presence. He comments: "You have not let me know whom you will send with me. . . . If your presence does not go with us, do not send us up from here" (Exod. 33:12, 15). Rightly or wrongly, Moses feels alone in his situation. With the possible exception of the young Joshua, everyone appears to have fallen short.

It's worth reminding ourselves that Aaron (Moses' own brother, for heaven's sake!) had just failed Moses (as well as the people—and God). His effort at guiding the unstable people of Israel in Moses' absence had been disastrous. How could he be much of a "presence"?

Does Moses' comment in the tent indicate that he is becoming increasingly aware that any venture that is sacred needs a sense of presence much greater than what any "mere man" can provide?

"Who will you send with me?" Moses asks. And God answers, "My presence will go with you, and I will give you rest."

I love those words. They seem to assure Moses that he need never panic; he can depend upon the presence of almighty God, the rescuer.

This same promise would be affirmed over and over again to leaders that God would call into service long after Moses: *I will be with you.* Sacred presence. And it is repeated in the promise of Jesus to the apostles, "I am with you always, even to the end of the age" (Matt. 28:20 NLT).

Some questions worth pondering: What does it feel like to experience the presence of God? How would you distinguish such an experience from all other experiences?

Direction and Purpose

Moses' second agenda in the tent has to do with direction and purpose. "Teach me your ways," he asks (Exod. 33:13). In other words, "What are your intentions for these people and me?" These are the words of a leader who needs clarification of God's purposes at a far deeper level than just budgets and program planning.

"This nation is your people [not mine!]," Moses reminds God. It's almost as if he's saying, "I've taken my best shot, and it's hard for me to find much that is redeemable about these people." I hear him saying: "They are *your* people, God. I can't handle them. So tell me, what is it that you intend for all of us?"

Moses' cry for further illumination reminds me of how often, as a young pastor, I would become confused by all the invitations and advertisements concerning conferences and seminars that promised to make my ministry a high-octane, revival-level experience. Everyone, it seemed, had a program for my leadership life.

Dr. Howard Hendricks came to visit, and I confessed to him my bewilderment in knowing how, with all the options before me, I was to lead our church. His words were instructive and reassuring: "Whatever the choice of direction may be, it starts not by reading the promises in the magazines or brochures but by settling the important things first on your knees. Cultivate the ability to hear God speak about these things."

He was right. While Hendricks' words did not solve the entire problem, they spelled out my first priority, which Moses illustrates. A leader has to remain on his or her knees until God has spoken. And when you are young and energetic, that is difficult to do.

In Moses' case, God did speak: "I will do the very thing you have asked, because I am pleased with you and I know you by name" (Exod. 33:17). Moses got what he asked for: a guarantee that if everything else fell apart, he, Moses, would remain in the crosshairs of God's pleasure and assurance. Just because people are responding poorly does not mean God is displeased with the leader.

Glory

Moses also asks: "Show me your glory." Glory equals power, and in this context, I think Moses is seeking a greater appraisal of God's capability. Has he forgotten about the powerful initiatives of God in previous months? Maybe not.

But Moses, like us, is human, and it's tomorrow he's worried about. As they get further away from the site of the original miracles, does Israel's God still have the power it takes to overcome the gods of the tribes and nations they will face? Can God's power hold this herd of "cats" called Israel together? Can God keep Moses going?

This question of power and its source is worthy for today's Christian leaders too. Can leaders become overconfident in the new ministry schemes, the technologies, the hype that flows today? Can we reach a point where we become jaded and slowly lose interest in this core issue of spiritual power that comes from God, and God alone?

In the apparent lessening of teaching on one's total reliance upon God's Spirit, is there a dangerous growth in a private self-confidence that rises out of modern management techniques, technology, charisma, and celebrity ministry?

I see Moses clamoring for a renewal of confidence in God's glory and power; I see him realize that he is struggling. He isn't sure that this Promised Land vision is going to work unless he is reenergized by a vision of God's glory. The disappointments of the last days have been so devastating that he is almost back to square one: those days before the burning bush.

How kind of God to patiently remind him with an apparent display of power. "I will cause all my goodness to pass in front of you, and I will proclaim my name, the LORD, in your presence. I will have mercy on whom I will have mercy, and I will have compassion on whom I will have compassion" (Exod. 33:19).

Meaning? "Moses, these Hebrews are a messy people. But my mercy and compassion begin with people who are capable of being the worst of the worst. That, apparently, is Israel in all its faithlessness. The power of God lies not necessarily in an ability to overwhelm armies and their generals; it begins first with an even greater power: to redeem hopeless people who dance around golden calves (or whatever) the minute they get a chance."

That's what transpired when Moses went to the tent. When he came out, he knew three things: God was with him, God had great purposes, and God was adequate to the situation. I suppose he also learned again that he was God's man for the hour.

You learn those kinds of things in such "tents." And that has served to stabilize me in most of the moments in my life when quitting seemed an attractive option.

I read Moses' story the morning after that first church business meeting that went sour. And I've read it many times since. It never stops speaking to me.

And it occurs to me, then, to ask this question of every reader who has gotten this far: Where is your tent? And when was the last time you entered it?

FOR FURTHER REFLECTION

1. *How do you describe your "tent" (see p.141)? When you feel spiritually attacked, what stabilizes you?*

2. *In prayer, what promises has God made to you? What have you specifically asked him for, and how has he answered your request?*

3. *How would you define God's power, and where do you see it at work in today's world? In your world?*

SAYING THE HARD STUFF

For I wrote you out of great distress and anguish of
heart and with many tears, not to grieve you but
to let you know the depth of my love for you.

2 CORINTHIANS 2:4

One of the first pastors of the church in Ephesus, Timothy, apparently didn't like the hard stuff side of ministry. And that worried his mentor, Paul, considerably and explains much of the content of the two letters written to Timothy in the New Testament.

Ephesus was a tough city, and the Ephesian Christians were tough people—many of them freshly converted out of unspeakably dark spiritual conditions. My suspicion is that Timothy found Ephesus and its Christians a bit more than he could handle and wanted out. Perhaps that explains why Paul begins the correspondence by saying, "Stay there!"

Apparently, Timothy was a nice and gentle young man. "I have no one else like Timothy," Paul wrote the Philippians, "who genuinely cares about your welfare" (Phil. 2:20 NLT). Quite a compliment.

But he seemed to struggle with the hard stuff. I'm talking about the kind of preaching and discipling that exposes errant belief, sinful attitudes, and ungodly behavior. Hard stuff: calling people to sacrificial living. Hard stuff makes people squirm; sometimes it makes them angry. But it may cause them to be repentant and eager to find better ways.

Timothy seems similarly reluctant in personal pastoral conversations. Although he was good at eliciting how people feel, where they hurt, where they are struggling (and many pastors do this well), he may have backed off from the confrontations necessary to expose people's sin and destructive behavior. One of the earlier hard-stuff messages in the Bible was God's to Cain: "Sin is waiting to attack and destroy you, and you must subdue it" (Gen. 4:7 NLT). Paul is wishing he heard more of that from Timothy.

Preach hard stuff (in Timothy's day as well as ours), and you run the risk that people will leave the church—or make the preacher leave the church! I am reminded of the cartoon in which the preacher says to his wife, "I told them the truth, and they set me free." Admittedly, preaching hard stuff risks losing friends, lowering financial giving—and attendance.

Timothy, it appears, softened rather than toughened his words when he needed to. There are hints that he was guided by his fears, that he had a weak stomach, that he quickly gave ground when he was challenged. Paul—no stranger to these issues—puts it bluntly: "Timothy, stop it! Grow up! Be the 'prophet' God called you to be! Don't let anyone back you into a corner."

People Pleasers

There is a subtle snare for us "nice guys." We don't like to be hurt, and we don't like to hurt others. We love unity, harmony, and happiness in the body. And we drift into the trap of thinking that the best way to achieve that is to avoid the hard stuff.

I bet Timothy spent sleepless nights brooding on anyone who criticized his leadership or opposed his efforts. I imagine he tried to woo people back into his favor. And—I'm just guessing here—that he was tempted to pull punches when preparing sermons whenever he realized that a certain comment might offend key people in the congregation.

Early in my own ministry, a board chairman whom I loved and respected became exasperated with me. "Pastor," he said one day, "you have a problem! You're too sensitive. You don't want to hear tough words, and you don't want to speak them when they need to be said. You'd better resolve this, or you're not going to last in the ministry." Paul lives!

Read Paul's two letters to Timothy, and you may get the feeling that Timothy's over-the-top "people sensitivities" were driving Paul nuts. Kind of like my board chairman. That's why the older man challenges the young man so powerfully: "Convince, rebuke, exhort, correct, don't let older people intimidate you or blow you off, don't be timid, guard your gospel carefully, and don't let anyone whittle it down" (cf. 1 Tim. 4).

Paul was right, of course. Hard stuff was needed from the pastor at Ephesus because the people lived in a culture saturated with arrogance, violence, greed, stinginess, immorality, and (if that weren't enough) blatant paganism. And these influences are not easily erased from the redeemed soul.

Preaching hard stuff was needed because the Ephesian congregation was not distinguished by qualities of spiritual beauty. Gossip and slander abounded, wannabe-teachers and leaders competed for recognition and control, and indications are that there was a dimension of church life that moderns identify as spiritual warfare. It wasn't imagined; it was real.

Paul was not asking Timothy to do anything he himself hadn't done many times. His letters to the Corinthians, for example, are full of hard stuff. He challenges dumb-downed theology and expresses consternation about the evils of disunity and insensitivity. He takes on the issues of in-church immorality, of destructive hero-worship. He is blunt about misused spiritual gifts, and he calls out the Corinthians for their dismal record of financial generosity.

Nowhere in the Corinthian letters are these issues candy-coated; nowhere are they compromised for fear of alienating people. Paul is Paul. You hear him saying, "Here's the truth, and let it sting and cleanse where it has to."

Mishandled Hard Stuff

This is not to say that Paul enjoyed delivering hard stuff. Unlike some, then and now, he was not a homiletical sadist. I think I have heard a few who are. Hard stuff is their only brand. They don't feel that a sermon is a sermon if it doesn't make people angry, raise guilt, or feel as if they are the only "pure" ones in the world (everyone else being so wicked). Preaching nothing but hard stuff is a subtle way to control people.

Crazy as it seems, such preachers can appeal to a kind of people who love hard stuff, who don't feel that they have heard the Word of God if it isn't razor-edged with anger and accusation.

These kinds of preachers and audiences seem to find each other (the sadist and the masochist). Preachers who preach nothing but hard stuff are usually angry people themselves. They love throwing their opinions around like hand grenades.

In spite of what my board chairman said about my supersensitivity, I did dabble in hard stuff from time to time. And there *was* feedback.

One day, when I was very new to preaching, the father of one of our families stormed into my little office after a sermon in which I had told the parents of our teenagers that their parenting skills were inadequate. At the time, of course, I had no children of my own, a fact that he pointed out. He brought information that refuted some "facts" with which I'd whacked people. And, finally, he wished to inform me about some realities in child-rearing I couldn't have known apart from first-hand experience.

He certainly got my attention. The episode made me evaluate how I preached hard stuff and what its effect might be. I couldn't be insensitive or (in this case) poorly informed. Doing your homework (both spiritual and intellectual) is necessary before you deal with hard stuff.

I wince when I remember the day I made a papal-like pronouncement on divorce and later learned that seated near the front was a church member's daughter who hadn't been in worship for years but who had come fresh from the divorce court, seeking consolation for her shattered life.

Oh, and there was the day I chose to speak on sacrificial stewardship when several men had just lost their jobs that week.

What I missed was the fact that hard stuff is more than just telling people how off course they are. What I had to learn is what parents have to learn: You don't earn the confidence of your children if all you do is hammer them with critical comments. When it has to happen—and it does—preach hard stuff like a shepherd who would give his life for the sheep.

Blending Anger and Affection

When Paul wrote hard stuff to Corinth, he made it clear that this was not easy for him. "I write to you tearfully," he said (cf. 2 Cor. 2:4). These are not the words of a man just venting anger and frustration at people who have let him (or the Lord) down. They are the words of a tender father who writes out of brokenheartedness because he loves his people so much.

When Paul raised hard stuff, it was with dignity and exemplary candor. "I can't treat you as spiritually-oriented people. . . . I have to treat you like children, offering you milk instead of meat" (cf. 1 Cor. 3:2). How's that for bluntness? But later he will remind his hearers that the words were for their benefit. "Some of you are becoming arrogant . . . some of you are actually proud that there is a bit of immorality among you . . . some of you who are pursuing lawsuits with each other are defeated already" (cf. 1 Cor. 4–5). This is hard stuff, and Paul does not hold back. However, it's surgery with a clean, sharp knife.

And then: "I don't regret for a moment that I wrote [hard stuff] to you even if it caused you sorrow" (cf. 2 Cor. 7:8).

Or this: "I am afraid that when I come next to visit you I will be greatly distressed by what I find" (cf. 2 Cor. 12:20).

What I like about these lines is that Paul talks frankly but without dismissing the Corinthians. "I'm angry with you," I hear him saying, "but my anger is fueled by my affection for you."

It was not only the Corinthians who heard hard stuff from Paul. To the Galatians he wrote: "You foolish [people]: who has deceived you? . . . I wish those who are obsessed with circumcision would concentrate on emasculating themselves" (cf. Gal. 3).

To the Colossians he wrote: "See to it that no one takes you captive through hollow and deceptive philosophy, which depends on human tradition and the basic principles of this world rather than on Christ" (Col. 2:8). A search for all of Paul's hard stuff could take hours.

Elizabeth O'Connor once overheard her nieces playing school. The oldest of the three, Lisa, played the teacher and said, "Now, children, there is no such thing as an Easter bunny. Do you hear me?"

One of the "students" protested: "Lisa, Lisa, stop teaching us things we do not want to hear!"

148

This is the crux of the issue when it comes to hard stuff. It usually means subject matter that people do not want to hear. So the pastor had better be on solid ground when hard-stuff time comes.

Solid Ground

You are on solid ground when you begin with a careful handling of Scripture. I'm not talking about proof texts where one starts with an opinion and then seeks some sort of biblical endorsement. But a search of the Bible with these kinds of questions:

- What does the Bible say about this issue?

- Which biblical people dealt with this matter and why?

- What are the implications if we do not change—or if we do?

As preachers, we are on solid ground when we have sought the insights of deep thinkers of the Christian movement, not just from our generation but from earlier ones. This means time in the library, of course. How have they spoken to these matters? How did their conclusions affect people in their time? (Become doubly aware when you learn that some were burned at the stake when they said hard stuff.)

Does it need to be said that solid ground also means getting our facts straight? Too often, preachers get away with unsubstantiated generalities ("62 percent of men are . . . 84 percent of churches are doing . . . 40 percent of Americans say . . .") that they heard somewhere on a radio broadcast or in some conversation. Surgical preaching that cuts out spiritual disease demands unimpeachable information.

Solid ground also comes out of a deep and searching prayer life. Prayer, first, that one is operating out of a heart of love; that one is not seeking to control or punish; that one seeks only God's best for people. I think our people do not hear enough today that we have been on our knees interceding for them. That alone will concentrate the minds of more than a few in our congregation.

Solid ground means examining our heart to see if what we're saying comes from a deep affection and priestly concern for the person in the pew. Am I in touch with the realities of the real-world life and the pressures people are facing?

In comparing two preachers who preached on hell, a listener said, "The one preached about hell as if he were glad some of us were going there. But the other preached as if the thought that anyone might go there was breaking his heart."

Finally, solid ground requires an integrity check. If I am about to say tough things to my people, it is wise to make sure that I am not under the same judgment I'm about to offer. And if I am, then I must let them know that this is an issue "with which we are all—beginning with myself—struggling."

Hard stuff may include thoughts that are counter to the majority political opinions of a congregation. Hard stuff may mean warning people of an arrogant and condemning spirit toward those who have differing positions on various moral and social issues. And hard stuff may mean calling to our listeners' attention the vast number of things the Christian movement tends to ignore because the cultural status quo protects our interests.

Within the church itself, hard stuff may mean holding up the biblical mirror and challenging people to measure themselves in the light of Christ's purity and call to a holier life. It may mean challenging people on the genuineness of their conversion or their blindness to behaviors that are offending and dividing others.

Say What Must Be Said

One time, I felt constrained to preach to my congregation about the growth of a polarizing spirit over a particular issue. People were talking too much, aligning themselves around positions that were causing strain on fellowship. Unnecessary, hurtful words were being spoken, and good people, feeling angry, were on the verge of going separate ways.

I began the sermon with two personal stories. I first shared with them a moment in my life when I wrongfully held a spirit of resentment against another person. I described the battle I had gone through to forgive. Then I told a second story of a time when someone had resented me. Here I described what it felt like to be on the other end of the stick.

When I had the attention of the congregation, I said quietly, "And it is out of my experience on those two occasions that I have a deep and prayerful concern for each of you today." From there I developed a biblical model for the matter we faced.

On the other end of that teaching, I faced the current issue squarely: "I am terribly disappointed in what I'm seeing and hearing today, and (with my voice lowered) it . . . needs . . . to . . . stop . . . right now! I'm not asking you to do anything I haven't had to do in my own journey: Stop hurting each other. Start forgiving each other. The next time I get evidence that this kind of thing is happening, I will come straight to you and raise the matter on a personal basis."

Because I am too much like Timothy, this was very hard to do. But much of the problem was resolved over the next few days.

How often my father said to me when I was a misbehaving child and he was compelled to punish me, "This hurts me more than it hurts you." As a child, I found this claim preposterous.

Today I understand it. It says well what the preacher's heart should be saying: "When it comes to hard stuff, the greater pain is in the soul of the one in the pulpit who must speak tenderly but candidly."

That was Timothy's struggle. It has been mine. Perhaps it is yours too.

FOR FURTHER REFLECTION

1. *Would you describe yourself more as a Timothy or a Paul?*

2. *Think back to a time in your life when you had to say "hard stuff" to someone. How did you approach this, and what was the outcome?*

3. *How can you make sure that you are on solid ground when you are required to share hard stuff? How much time do you spend studying Scripture, praying, and reading the writings of deep Christian thinkers, past and present?*

DNF: DID NOT FINISH

So, if you think you are standing firm,
be careful that you don't fall!

1 CORINTHIANS 10:12

When you read the results of a race—be it cars, people, or animals—it's not unusual to see DNF attached to some entrants' names. The letters—standing for Did Not Finish—indicate those who had to quit. Sometimes the reason is also indicated: a blown engine, for example, a pulled muscle, or lameness.

What if the equivalent to a DNF were put by the name of every seminary graduate who is now doing something other than the ministry they once felt called to? Every study of dropouts I hear about suggests that it would be an enormous list.

If reasons were affixed, you might read stress and burnout, conflict, inadequate people skills, insufficient leadership capability, poor work habits, family unhappiness, or mean-spirited congregants. There would be many others, of course.

And among those would be one that would probably catch your eye the fastest: moral failure. The term arouses a lot of natural curiosity and not a little apprehension. The mind wonders: *What happened? Why? How was it discovered? What has happened to the people involved? Could this happen to me?*

The term *moral failure* covers a broad spectrum of tragic conduct. Someone has acknowledged an attraction to pornography; another is discovered to have engaged in an improper relationship (with either gender); still a third is found to have a history of some kind of molestation. Is this list large enough?

Given Jesus' sweeping definition of adultery (the intents of the heart), I suppose we are all moral failures in one way or another. Murderers, too. Some in Christian leadership go beyond the intents of the heart and act out them out. Almost every time, an unspeakable heartbreak ripples out into many lives. Beyond that, there is always disillusionment, scorn, and the loss of trust that accompanies such sin. Sins of the flesh are destructive and usually result in a DNF.

As much as I dislike the term *moral failure,* I am going to stick with it here. And I'm going to stipulate right now that moral failure is inexcusable, destructive, shameful, a matter of disgrace, and downright sinful. I think most of us would agree.

Of all the things I have written, this subject is the most difficult—one I would like to have avoided—because I know too much. Years ago, I was guilty of moral failure, and, along with my wife, I have talked to many others who were as well. I can tell you that the issue and its causes and solutions cannot be adequately addressed in a matter of a few thousand words. One can only scratch the surface. Every situation is unique; every situation has to be dealt with differently.

Prevailing Temptations

Years ago, when I lived in New York City and pastored a church heavily populated by people in the financial world, I came to realize that *greed* was a major theme among those who handle money. Money—there was never enough of it, and some bent all the rules to get more.

When I had the opportunity to mix it up in Washington, DC, with so-called politicians, I saw that *power* was a similar problem. There is never enough power in Washington, and many lust after it and cut corners to gain it.

Having lived in New England for a large part of my adult life, I have also seen something of the sins of *knowledge*, of intellectual arrogance. The brilliant folks of the Ivy League world may not always be the richest (wealth) or the most powerful (politics), but they can be among the most prideful—brutally so.

My point is this: What money is to the financial folks, and power is to political people, and knowledge is to intellectuals, *intimacy*—deep connections with people—is to those of us who are in the people business (pastors, spiritual directors, therapists, psychologists, counselors).

A preponderant percentage of those of us drawn to pastoral leadership have a higher-than-normal urge to engage with other people. We love to get below the surface of people's exterior lives: to understand their dreams and their burdens, to urge them on to higher possibilities, to sympathize with their feelings and fears, to show them grace and mercy when they fail. The word *close* is operational here.

When we get this "up-close-and-personal" with people, we come within sight of behaviors that cross the boundary into the inappropriate. The so-called temptations of the flesh become prominent under such circumstances and among people who operate in a world of intimacies.

This is not a problem if those in leadership are mature, balanced, self-aware, humble, sin-sensitive people who live in healthy and open accountability. But whoever said that these things would be true of all of us?

In ministry, we are often given privileges and liberties that are nice—but dangerous. We are given responsibilities that carry influence and power and invite adulation in that small social set called the congregation (or subsets of it). People give us respect and attention in ways they extend to few others. They form a fantasy about who we are: godly, spiritually mature, compassionate, sensitive, nearly perfect. Oh, and it should be said, they often abandon these perspectives sooner or later and can drop us with a thud.

Unless a leader is very (very!) careful, this can become an environment that distorts reality and engenders confusion of mind and heart in any number of ways. It accentuates loneliness, for example. *Who are my real friends?* the leader asks. *Why do I feel as if everyone owns a piece of me and there is nothing left for myself? Who really knows the real me? Who is there that doesn't want something from me? Why do I always have to worry about what others think?*

Such thoughts intensify if the leader feels seriously misunderstood or unappreciated. Take it a step further if the leader also feels unappreciated, disrespected, or misunderstood in his or her home and marriage.

This unreal environment is not helped by the tendency for there to be a contrived intimacy in human relations in a church. It can be a place where we share our secrets under the guise of prayer requests or counseling. It is easy for strangers to touch ("Let's form a prayer circle and hold hands"), or to say things to each other without the benefit of months or years of the normal growth of friendship. We praise and thank one another (calling it "affirmation"), and we do so in ways that can easily invite the crossing of personal boundaries that are not normally done in the larger world. These are all ways for leaders and followers to get the wrong idea about another's intentions.

It is not a far distance from a prayer circle to a cup of coffee for two where crossing into impropriety begins. Suddenly, someone feels understood, appreciated, and admired in ways that are not happening in more appropriate relationships or settings. Note the emphasis upon the word *feels*. You hear stories that begin with words like these: "We jogged together at the park"; "She was helping me develop my Power-Point presentations"; "He was repairing our furnace."

In short—and I mean no disrespect—the church with its emphasis on being transparent, vulnerable, and authentic can easily be a seed-bed for moral failure, especially for leaders. It is far better to overstate this than understate the possibility.

From Intimacy to Sex

If most pastors have a greater instinct for intimate connections with people, then it does not surprise me that some (mostly male) pastors will be attracted to various pornographic exposures in which intimacy is simulated and where there is—for a brief period of time—a sense of the kind of inner satisfaction that genuine intimacy is supposed to produce.

Just as alcohol or drugs can produce a pseudo-sense of well-being, of personal freedom, of pain-freeness for a short while, so pornography is capable of offering a momentary high not dissimilar to that experienced when there is genuine intimacy between two lovers.

The insidious nature of pornography, as almost everyone knows, is that it is a private event in most cases, capable of being carried out in secrecy. It is exposed only when one is surprised in the act, or when the person becomes so overcome by guilt that he feels compelled to confess it and seek help. Usually by this time the problem has reached addictive proportions, and dealing with it becomes very difficult.

Others in ministry have reached the DNF column not through pornography but by engaging in relationships that violate the terms of marriage or biblical standards of propriety.

Enmeshment describes something I fear happens more than anyone could ever realize. The word describes a connection between two people (unmarried or not married to each other) who work together in ministry and become dependent upon one another for emotional support. The nature of their activities (leader and assistant; ministry teammates; leader and volunteer; pastor and counselee) leads to levels of conversation and teamwork that puncture the healthy boundaries that normally separate us from one another.

Again, this possibility is accentuated if one or both parties have unstable relationships at home: an untended marriage that has lost its focus, or where there is a lack of mutual support. I often hear my wife say that it is human to move toward the strokes, those places and people where the greatest encouragement, the greatest sense of understanding can be found.

I have talked to too many men in ministry who have morally failed, who have said to me, "I never got into this relationship with the intention of sexual activity. I simply found the friendship of this person to be more satisfying than what I was finding with my spouse." The sexual part came afterward . . . like a trap that was sprung from within the human heart. It doesn't start with sexual activity; it starts with something else that seems quite innocent.

Consider another dimension in the well-rehearsed story of David and Bathsheba. Like many who ascend to leadership positions, David, as king, might have gradually begun to live above the rules that others are expected to follow. The responsibilities and pressures of leadership often do a number on the mind of the leader. One slowly convinces himself or herself that there are privileges and freedoms that should be given (if not seized) because "I am so valuable to this organization and its work."

At first, the privileges are defended because they make leadership life easier or more effective. A private parking space is a good example:

it's time-saving, leader-honoring, a perk of the work, a symbol of one's authority. A larger office, a private bathroom, more vacation time? All very appropriate for those leading larger organizations and churches, but this can become an elixir of perceived indispensability.

All of this begins to erode the soul's vigilance and tempts a leader to set aside moral rules and boundaries (perhaps just once, the self-deceiving mind says). The abilities of our minds to engage in self-justification are amazing and downright frightening.

In the aftermath of his sin, David appears to be oblivious of the seriousness of what has happened with Bathsheba. He goes on running the country as if nothing untoward has happened. Her husband is a problem? Find a way to cover things up—even if it means his death. When confronted by Nathan, it is clear that David cannot, at first, face the truth. It must be put into story form so that he can get it on his own.

It is often said that leadership is lonely. There is truth to this, of course, but if it is lonely, it may indeed be the leader's fault. While a leader may bear some unique responsibilities, part of a leader's job is to build in appropriate amounts of time for the pursuit of family/marital priorities and for enjoying some same-gender personal friendships.

It is not unusual for a leader to experience distance between him (here I use male terminology with apologies) and his spouse. It can be an intellectual distance if he grows in different ways than she does. It can be a distance created when he invests more time and energy in his work and she (for various reasons) less. The distance can be one of adulation where he is more and more praised for success and she begins to drop into the shadows of his private life.

At the same time, others of the opposite gender may come closer to him because they are more closely aligned in the work side of his life. A new kind of "togetherness" occurs because they share prime-time hours where one is at his or her supreme points of competence, where the intoxication of vision and accomplishment is shared. New, perhaps unhealthy, sinews of relationship are formed at just the same time as the original sinews of a marital relationship are weakening. The possible results are not hard to imagine.

The Internal War

I find it hard to put into clinical words what I intuit. Simply put, I am not confident that many young men and women entering public ministry with all of its privileges and demands are emotionally (and spiritually?) ready to face the subtleties of human relationships on their darker side.

I am also not sure that many midlife men and women appreciate all the pressures bearing down on them that make it easy to seek illicit ways to anesthetize the growing discomfort within. Saying good-bye to children, adjusting to a now childless marriage, caring for aging parents, facing the inexorable aging process with its health issues: pressure, pressure, pressure! For the less vigilant, escape into something simpler, more exciting, and seemingly more fun can be exceedingly attractive.

The pastoral task—relative to many other jobs—is not submitted to adequate systems of accountability. In a sense, we send men and women out to do a job that is not unlike sending soldiers into battle. Just as there was a scandal in the Iraq war where soldiers had inadequate armor, so too the armor of many in ministry is inadequate.

We do not respect the darkness of the human heart in such a way that we believe the finest and best of our leaders could—overnight— capitulate to temptations that they themselves once thought powerless.

In my book, *Rebuilding Your Broken World*, I told the story of a man I met at a conference. I could tell he was trying to create conversation as he asked: "How do you think Satan could blow you out of the water?" I was a younger man at the time and had no quick answer. So

I said, "I'm not sure, but I am confident that he could never get at me by undermining my personal relationships." I could hardly have said a more foolish thing. A few years later, I was a potential DNF, and it was reasonable to ask if I would ever "race" again. Why? For a moment, I had failed in the one human relationship most important to me.

As pastoral life grows more intense with greater demands and expectations, I do not believe the so-called moral failures of leaders will subside. I fear they will increase, and we will hear of more good leaders with DNF by their names. Just writing this makes me sad.

Perhaps these changes could stem the tide:

1. Let's stop beating around the bush about moral temptations and talk about them in the same way a commanding officer talks about the dangers of going into battle. The officer does not assume that anyone is exempt from taking a bullet, so all are forewarned.

2. Let's require that every man and woman in Christian leadership belong to a peer-oriented group that creates covenants of behavior, such as no casual dining with a member of the opposite sex, no travel of any kind with colleagues of the opposite sex, and no team relationships unless three or more people are involved.

3. Let's make sure every pastor and spouse has a mentoring couple who keeps an inquiring eye upon family and marital life and steps in if they believe that systems of healthy relationships are breaking down.

4. Let's be more honest about the high-risk effects of ministry in large churches: what happens to marriages, mental and emotional health, and spiritual vitality. We're doing great in teaching about vision-casting, outreach, management, and leadership. But—I'll be as blunt as I can—we are failing miserably to help young men and women form the necessary soul-power to undergird those efforts.

5. Let's frankly admit the fact that, in our contemporary Christian culture, we are—most of us—starved for healthy intimacy at every level and, when we do not experience it, we are likely to turn toward

the sexual to find it. We need to bring this to the surface, find ways to identify the drives and desires, and then talk about how to prevent it.

DNF—Did Not Finish: this is among the saddest of all epitaphs for a leader. Moral failure: this is among the most serious and tragic of the reasons. You would think we would talk more about this and what can be done to prevent it.

FOR FURTHER REFLECTION

1. *Have you been in a church or organization where a leader was involved in a scandal? How was this handled?*

2. *Have you yourself ever experienced a moral failure involving someone in your church or organization? If so, what steps did you take to rectify the situation?*

3. *If not, what steps have you taken to ensure that you will not inadvertently place yourself in the path of temptation?*

SOUL DEEP

O my brethren, my heart is enlarged towards you.
I trust I feel something of that hidden but powerful
presence of Christ whilst I am preaching to you.

GEORGE WHITEFIELD

"Wherever Paul traveled, revolutions broke out. Wherever I go, they serve tea." So said an Anglican bishop, lamenting his perceived lack of impact upon people.

We all know what he's saying, particularly in the area of preaching. You spend hours in preparation: both spiritual and scholastic. You seek stories and illustrations that ooze meaning and significance. You search your own life to make sure that you are as transparent as possible. Then, when the moment arrives, you preach your heart out. Words flow, thoughts build, stories produce laughter or reflective silence, decision time comes, and you expect ... Pentecost!

Moments later, the people file out with opaque comments such as "Nice sermon, Pastor," or "You gave me something to think about," or "You were really 'on' today."

On the drive home, your nerves are raw. Indeed, it was a nice morning, but did anything happen? Like a revolution, for example? Or did we just serve our usual tea?

I've made that trip home countless times. I've entered the pulpit feeling that I possessed the spirit of a John Wesley, and I've come out of the pulpit feeling like Cedric the Entertainer. It's a blue moment.

Powerful Preachers

Preaching the Bible seems, at first glance, always to have provoked powerful reactions. Ezra and the Levites, for instance, taught the Law to the people, and the crowd could not stop weeping. Imagine being John the Baptist when the crowds cried out, "What shall we do?" Then there's Peter preaching at Pentecost, and the hearers are "cut to the heart." Paul preached at Philippi and "the Lord (opened) Lydia's heart." These are all impressive moments, which set a high expectation for any preacher.

Some speak of "anointed" or "Spirit-filled" preaching as they reflect on the origin of preaching power. On the other end of the transaction, where words are received by the listener, I would describe it as *soul-deep preaching*.

Soul-deep preaching is several steps beyond brain-deep preaching, or feelings-deep preaching, or guilt-deep preaching. The former provokes conviction, conversion, brave new actions. The rest produce a momentary experience of good feelings or an intellectual appreciation of a solid point well made—but not much more.

An old cartoon features one preacher saying to another, "When you come right down to it, I'm just a collection of clichés, but I think I've managed to combine them in a rather exciting way." That's probably not said by a soul-deep preacher.

Soul-deep sermons reflect the description of the "Word of God" in Hebrews 4:12: "It penetrates even to dividing soul and spirit, joints and marrow; it judges the thoughts and attitudes of the heart." You don't get any deeper than that.

It's important to observe that not all biblical preaching struck the soul, apparently. Take the words God spoke to Ezekiel: "Your countrymen are talking together about you . . . saying to each other, 'Come and hear the message that has come from the LORD.' My people come to you, as they usually do, and sit before you to listen to your words, but they do not put them into practice. With their mouths they express devotion, but their hearts are greedy for unjust gain. Indeed, to them you are nothing more than one who sings love songs with a beautiful voice . . . for they hear your words but do not put them into practice" (Ezek. 33:30–32).

Sounds like a pretty resistant crowd to me, people beyond "convictability" (a word I think I've coined).

Those of us who are called to preaching long to deliver soul-deep sermons. We hear of preaching moments where scads of people responded to Jesus Christ or opened their lives to God's love. And we want God to use us similarly.

Of course, that kind of preaching—the soul-deep kind—does not necessarily invite the kind of praise that satisfies the ego. But it might instigate various kinds of revolutions. Change of heart, change of mind, change of attitude, change in relationships, change of behavior. It elicits worship, repentance, gratitude, submission. It might galvanize people to march together in new directions with a fresh sense of kingdom purpose.

Our Role in the Soul

When I reflect on soul-deep preaching as I've read about it, seen it happening, and—dare I say—experienced it (a few times), some thoughts come to mind.

Let me start with the obvious: *Soul-deep preaching is an act of God.* It shouldn't (and probably couldn't anyway) be reduced to mechanics or techniques. "Stand up and say to them whatever I command you," God said to a young Jeremiah (Jer. 1:17).

A soul-deep sermon can come from the lips of a simple, stammering, uneducated person, or from the heart and mind of a Rhodes scholar. God is not limited when vetting his messengers. Intellectually, Paul was at the top of his class; Peter was a working man. But both were tops in the soul-deep preaching department. Go figure.

But the person does matter. We do not live in a day when a person can separate from the crowd and assume something like an actor's persona at pulpit time. We are talking about a believable person whose personal holiness and practical faith are clear to see in the nooks and crannies of real life.

Gerald Kennedy quotes Luther: "When I preach in the Stadtkirche, I stoop down. I do not look up to the doctors and the masters of arts, of whom there are about forty in my audience, but I look upon the crowd of young people, children, the servants, of whom there are several hundred. To them I preach. To them I adapt myself. They need it. If the doctors don't care to hear that style of preaching, the door is open for them to leave."

I was twenty-seven years of age, a senior in seminary, when I was asked to preach in a Baptist church in St. Paul, Minnesota. A few moments before I was to go to the pulpit, the host pastor suddenly leaned over and whispered, "See those guys in the second and third row? That's most of the Bethel Seminary faculty."

I felt the inner regions of my abdominal area rearrange, for the folks in the second and third row were a formidable, austere-looking bunch. *What in the world,* I asked myself, *could I conceivably say to such a group that would compel their attention?* Luther's words would have helped me at that moment.

Then I heard what seemed to be a direct message from heaven: "Don't preach; just talk from your heart to them about what you've been hearing me say. You're prepared; you're ready; just talk to them."

A moment later I stood up and talked, quietly, personally, and as sincerely as I knew how. I didn't pretend that I was anything more than a twenty-seven year old who had been gripped by what the Scripture had to say.

"Talk to them." I've been trying to do that ever since. No stained-glass voice, no laundered vocabulary, no attempt to be much different than if we met in the Dunkin' Donuts line.

A. W. Tozer wrote fifty years ago:

There are preachers looked upon by their people as divine oracles, who wag their tongues all day in light, frivolous conversation. Then before entering the pulpit . . . [they] seek a last-minute reprieve in a brief prayer. Thereby they hope to put themselves into the position where the spirit of the prophet will descend upon them. It may be that by working themselves up to an emotional heat they may get by, may even congratulate themselves that they had liberty in preaching the Word. But they deceive themselves. What they have been all day and all week is what they are when they open up the Book to expound it to the congregation.

The Word Made Fresh

A soul-deep sermon has to do with one's insistence on taking scriptural truth and casting it in a twenty-first century frame—a challenging but not impossible task. Scholarship and imagination work together here to cultivate the curiosity of the congregation so that they are willing to crawl into the text with the preacher and appreciate why and how it was written and what the author was trying to say as he responded to the impulse of the Holy Spirit.

Having done that, it's down to work with the assumption that ancient truth is transcultural: it speaks to the present time. And what does it say? How will that truth translate into life on Tuesday or Thursday in the marketplace, in the home, or at school? What difference will it make? What does life for the biblical person look like?

I love to tell the story of a ferret named Bandit that our college-aged son brought home years ago. After some months, we had to ask Bandit to leave (behavioral problems), but no one could tell us how to appropriately evict him. When I suggested to the pet store people that we simply let Bandit go in the New Hampshire forest, they were horrified.

"He won't be able to defend himself or survive," they said. "He's trained to live in a cage."

We must beware of sermons that teach people to survive only in the protected cage of the church and among Christianized people. Soul-deep sermons take the powerful Gospel and place it in the context of the streets of this world where life is tough and people need courage and wisdom.

Urgency (I think we prefer the word *passion* today) is an interesting word when it comes to the consideration of soul-deep preaching. It is used to describe a preacher who really believes that the eternal destiny of human beings is caught up in the issues a sermon might address. This is a scary thought. Truth be told? I don't get the feeling that most preachers really believe that eternal issues are in the balance when they preach.

Readying the Crowd

There is the possibility of soul-deep sermons when congregations are prepared to listen at soul-depth. An Augustine, a Luther, a Calvin, a Wesley, a Spurgeon, and a Graham were effective when their audience was strangely ready. But here is an opposite case in point: "[Jesus] could not do any miracles there, except lay his hands on a few sick people and heal them. And he was amazed at their lack of faith" (Mark 6:5–6). So Mark writes of a day of preaching in the life of Jesus that could be labeled (forgive me, Lord) a strike-out.

A strange readiness, I say. Because there are times when God—for reasons we cannot understand—cracks through the hardness of souls and sends a sermon deep within. People repent; people change; people become, well . . . wonderful people. What readies a congregation? These moments are most often prefaced by large amounts of prayer.

A worshiper in a Welsh church back in 1859 writes of just such a moment when people would normally have been satisfied with a routine meeting.

> *[The pastor, having read some Scripture, made] a few passing remarks thereon, [and] an influence was felt by all present, which we had never experienced in the like manner before. There was a beauty, a loveliness about the holy Word which we had never hitherto perceived. New light seemed to be thrown upon it. It electrified us, and caused us to weep for joy. The feeling became general. All present were under its influence. The hardest hearts were forced to succumb . . . and then we sang, aye, sang with the Spirit, and repeated the hymn again and again—we could not leave off. Every heart seemed inspired to continue, and the last two lines were sung for full a quarter of an hour.*

Poof! The second Welsh revival was under way.

Results of Soul-Deep Preaching

We must not overload this idea of soul-deep preaching too much, but certainly some of the following attributes must be among its distinctive marks. A sense of the holiness and majesty of God might be one mark. This is a God with whom we must not trifle. He is to be respected and heard.

Then we might look for a sense of the deep, deep love of Jesus—a love that is virtually irresistible and which overcomes every barrier of the hardened soul. Jesus must be preached so that one cannot imagine living without a relationship with him.

Add to that the imperative of repentance. How could people leave a soul-deep sermon without being impressed with their unrighteousness and their need to make things right with God? Beyond that is the intent to change—a realization that this attitude or that conduct must be altered under the guidance and empowerment of the Holy Spirit.

One more result: The listener imagines a way to go out the door and make a difference in the name of Jesus: serve others; introduce someone to Jesus; right a wrong; protect a vulnerable person.

I wonder if soul-deep preaching isn't also characterized by a persuasive close. Salespeople use the word "close" to describe the moment when they ask a customer for a sale. Crass words for a preacher, but there does have to be a defined closure to a sermon, a clear description of the kind of response the preacher believes God expects. It has to be spelled out so that no one can escape the challenge.

Joshua was a great closer: "Choose for yourselves this day whom you will serve . . . As for me and my household, we will serve the LORD" (Josh. 24:15). He got a good response.

There is a spectrum in closing. At one end is the immediate response—when a preacher ends the sermon with an invitation. I like to do this occasionally, but I always warn people ahead of time. At the beginning of the sermon I say: "You need to know that at the end of this sermon I am going to give an invitation. It means that I'm going to invite you—if God is speaking into your life—to leave your seat, come to the front, and kneel and let someone pray for you. So as you listen to this sermon, keep in mind that I'm going to challenge every one of you to think through whether or not God is speaking and if you are one of those who should respond to my invitation."

I have never had such an invitation go without response. People so warned are people thinking with great seriousness. They come, and often it becomes a milestone in their spiritual journey.

At the other end of the spectrum is an open-ended response, tying a truth to something people will experience during the coming week. Here, the key is provocative questions or ideas that linger in their minds.

Not long ago, I preached a sermon on perseverance and quoted Yogi Berra, who said, "It's not over until it's over," and then made some appropriate applications. A few weeks later a couple approached me with a family story.

"Our ten-year-old daughter," they said, "was in a soccer game this week, and they were losing by a goal in the last five minutes. She heard the opposing team's coach say to his girls, 'It's almost over, and you're going to win.'"

After the game—which ended in a tie—she told her parents, "I heard that coach say that the game was almost over, and I remembered when Pastor Mac said, 'It's not over until it's over.' So I decided to play harder." She went on to score the tying goal.

Maybe that's not exactly the best illustration for soul-deep sermons, but if a ten year old can make a direct application days later, then anything is possible.

Remember Why You're There

The founder of the Quaker movement, George Fox, was a soul-deep preacher. When he reflected upon what made him this way, he simply answered, "I took men to Jesus Christ and left them there."

There was a time years ago when (I'm embarrassed to admit this) I grew a bit bored with preaching. While it was important to me to preach good sermons, I began to forget that there was a purpose behind it, that there were results to seek.

"I'm not sure that anyone is going to change because of what I say," I told my wife. "I need to remind myself to preach for change."

She heard me. And from that point forward, whenever I rose from my seat next to her to go to the pulpit, Gail would grab my arm as I stood up and say in a half-whisper, "Be a man sent from God; preach for change!"

She makes sure I remember the purpose of preaching.

FOR FURTHER REFLECTION

1. *In your own words, describe the difference between mediocre preaching and soul-deep preaching.*

2. *How important is it to "close" a sermon? What creative strategies have you used to call your listeners to action?*

3. *Think about someone you admire who has a depth of soul, whether in ministry or in business. What characterizes the way they live? the way they communicate?*

HOW A MIGHTY CHURCH FALLS

*Every institution, no matter how great, is vulnerable to
decline. Anyone can fall, and most eventually do. But
decline, it turns out, is largely self-inflicted, and the path
to recovery lies largely within our own hands. We are not
imprisoned by our circumstances, our history, or even our
staggering defeats along the way. As long as we never get
entirely knocked out of the game, hope always remains.
The mighty can fall, but they can often rise again.*

JIM COLLINS

Soon after I finished my theological education, I was asked to become pastor of a congregation in southern Illinois. This was my first
great awakening to the realities of pastoral leadership, and it was an
uncomfortable experience.

The skills (or gifts) that led the congregation to invite me to be
their spiritual leader were probably my enthusiasm, my preaching, and
my apparent ability, even as a young man, to reach out to people and
make them feel cared for.

The position called for me to report to a board of deacons who, while well-intentioned, were not highly experienced in organizational leadership. I was also responsible for leading a staff that consisted of a secretary, a Christian education assistant, two day-school teachers, a part-time choir director, and a janitor.

What the position description didn't say was that the congregation was seriously divided and disillusioned due to an acrimonious split in which the previous pastor had persuaded one hundred people to join him in leaving the church to form a new one down the road.

It took me only a couple of months to realize that I knew very little about how to lead an organization of such size, complexity, and woundedness. At age twenty-seven, I was in over my head. Somehow I had made it all the way through seminary believing that all one had to do was become a dazzling preacher and an enthusiastic visionary and everything else about church life would fall into place. No one told me about staffs that required direction, boards that wanted results, and congregations that needed healing.

I liken it to that discovery some young married couples make at the end of their honeymoon that, in addition to being affectionate and fun-loving, there are bills to pay, chores to share, and personality differences to resolve—all things they didn't realize were included in the marital package.

Churches and marriages have something in common: they are both organizations. One had better know how to run them. I didn't.

Organizational Leadership

It was in those "awakening" days that I was introduced to my first organizational leadership book: *The Effective Executive* by Peter Drucker. It became one of the most important books I ever read. It opened me up to understand how people are empowered to attain objectives that are otherwise unreachable. That book probably delivered me from a first-round knockout in my life as a pastor.

Since that time more than forty years ago, countless other writers have tried to improve upon Drucker's insights. In my opinion no one has succeeded quite like Jim Collins, who has given us books like *Good to Great* and *Built to Last*. I'm not sure that Collins had people like me in his crosshairs when he wrote those books, but many of us in faith-based and pastoral leadership have learned much from him.

Collins and his team of researchers also produced a smaller work entitled *How the Mighty Fall*, which he says began as an article and ended as a book. Being a preacher (and a writer), I understand that.

Collins says *How the Mighty Fall* was inspired by a conversation during a seminar at West Point where a few dozen leaders from the military, business, and social sectors gathered to explore themes of common interest. He had posed this question to the group: "Is America renewing its greatness, or is America dangerously on the cusp of falling from great to good?"

The conversation came during a break when one of the CEOs approached Collins to say: "I found our discussion fascinating, but I've been thinking all morning about your question in the context of my company. We've had tremendous success in recent years, and I worry about that."

The CEO went on to express the fear that success itself tends to cover the warning signs of decline. Therefore, he was haunted by the question: *How would you know that your organization is heading into trouble when things on the surface appear to be so good?*

That CEO now has his answer in the pages of *How the Mighty Fall*. Collins begins with a personal story that illustrates the point the book addresses. He describes a day when he and his wife, Joanne, went for a run on a mountain road near Aspen, Colorado. His wife, a well-conditioned runner, quickly outdistanced him, stopping only when she reached an altitude of almost thirteen thousand feet.

Yet a little more than two months later, Collins relates, she was diagnosed with cancer and faced two mastectomies. Collins' point: On the day of that run, his wife appeared to be the picture of health, but she must have already been carrying the growing disease within her.

"I've come to see institutional decline like a staged disease: harder to detect but easier to cure in the early stages, easier to detect but harder to cure in the later stages," writes Collins. "An institution can look strong on the outside but already be sick on the inside, dangerously on the cusp of a precipitous fall."

That reminds me of words written to the Laodicean church: "You say, 'I am rich; I have acquired wealth and do not need a thing.' But you do not realize that you are wretched, pitiful, poor, blind, and naked" (Rev. 3:17).

Five Stages of Decline

In the book, Collins identifies five stages in the process of organizational slippage. Each one, he suggests, is a section of that proverbial slippery slope that grows more dangerous as time goes on, and the problem is enhanced by the fact that, in most cases, leadership is apparently (or deliberately) oblivious to what is going on.

Any thoughtful organizational leader would want to know Collins' five stages well and would also want to make sure that his or her leaders were aware of them. What a menu they would be for a five-point discussion on a leadership retreat! When I first read them, I was impressed with how easy it was to match many of these observations to biblical descriptions of leadership and organizational life.

1. Hubris Born of Success

Take, for example, the first stage of organizational decline. Collins calls it "hubris born of success."

"We do ourselves a disservice by only studying success," writes Collins. A search and scan through the business and even church leadership literature suggests that few books explore the roots of failure. Most dote on promises of success.

Interestingly, the biblical writers are unafraid to write of failure. Mixed among the stories of great achievements in the Old and New Testaments are a host of accounts of personal and corporate failure.

Hubris—an arrogant conceit (Collins refers to it as "an excessive pride") that paves the way toward failure and its consequences—is found all over the Scriptures. I'm tempted to say that there may be more failure stories arising from hubris than success stories rising from humility.

For instance, Goliath and his fellow Philistines are full of hubris when the giant takes on David, the shepherd. David himself is later caught in the thrall of hubris when he gets into trouble with Bathsheba. Uzziah, a king of Israel for over fifty years, is nose-deep in hubris when, the Bible says, "he grew proud, to his destruction" (2 Chron. 26:16 ESV). In each of these cases, no one could conceive that anything under their control could go awry. There was simply an assumption that they deserved success, and they didn't consider any downside consequences.

Israel's national story is pockmarked with hubristic performances that open the door to humiliation and suffering. The shock of defeat at the small crossroads town of Ai, for example, happened not long after the stupendous victory at Jericho. No one before the battle of Jericho would have predicted Israel's success, and no one before the battle of Ai would have predicted Israel's defeat. Humility won Jericho; hubris lost Ai (cf. Josh. 8).

Hubris, a state of overconfidence in ourselves, our systems, and our successes, often makes leaders blind to points of weakness that are already bubbling up within an organization.

So it was with Ai. When spies scouted this two-bit town, they returned to Joshua and said, "Not all the army will have to go up against

Ai. Send two or three thousand men to take it and do not weary the whole army, for only a few people live there" (Josh. 7:3).

That's high-density hubris: Understate the problem; overstate your ability to accomplish.

By contrast, there is Acts 6:1. "But as the believers rapidly multiplied, there were rumblings of discontent" (NLT). This describes surface success while all the time a split-threatening issue is heating up underneath. It is to the apostles' credit that they quickly picked up on the situation and initiated a problem-solving process before things got worse.

After the horrific tsunami devastated many countries in the Pacific a few years ago, scientists began to plant sensors on the seabeds that could offer early warning of any seismic action that would generate tsunamis. Perhaps this is what organizational leaders must do. Find people, design specific indicators, identify spiritual "winds" that signal a problem is birthing: small now, but destined to enlarge if not addressed.

2. Undisciplined Pursuit of More

Collins admits that when he started to study organizational decline, he expected to find complacency at the root of most trouble. But he found that he was wrong. Overreaching (in some ways the opposite of complacency) turned out to be the real issue.

Overreaching is the undisciplined pursuit of growth accompanied by the neglect of those core principles upon which an organization was originally built. It's about getting larger and larger, more and more expansive, even if it costs the organization its soul.

I wonder if this is not a way of describing the problems of the Corinthian congregation. Paul's challenge to this organization is tinged with irony. Speaking of himself in self-deprecating, contrasting terms, he nails their overreach: "Already you have become rich . . . you have become kings . . . you are so wise . . . you are strong . . . you are honored" (cf. 1 Cor. 4:8–10).

Overreaching stems from a temptation to think that if we are good at what we're doing, we can do anything else just as successfully. This was the Corinthian situation.

Certain kinds of leaders, whether business or faith-based, become blinded by the elixir of expansion. All too often, it flows from the need of leaders to always be proving their self-worth, and they know no other way except to build larger and larger barns, no matter what the consequence.

It's the incessant idea that everything has to enlarge, grow larger, be more impressive. Consider Solomon, who as a youngish man ascended to the throne of his father, David. Early on, he was "smart" enough to recognize his need for "wisdom," and he prayed for it. God granted the request, and the early pages of Solomon's story are marked with amazing success.

But along the way, a pattern of personal overreach began. More horses and chariots, more money, more wives—in spite of the fact that Moses had warned in earlier days that a king in Israel ought to avoid all three and remind himself of their danger on a daily basis.

Putting it bluntly, Solomon migrated toward "more" and away from "wisdom." My bet is that if one of us had interviewed Solomon when he was at the peak of his career, he would have had airtight, maybe even theological, reasons for his expansion. Perhaps his rationale would have silenced the best of us. But his overreach ultimately led to his decline. We wonder: why did this wise man have to have more and more and more? And why did Israel have to suffer as a result?

Are there Solomonic overreaches in our time?

I'm impressed that Jesus' charge to the apostles had much more to do with making disciples than building larger organizations. He seems to have known that properly trained platoons of disciples in every town and village would take care of the movement and keep it cleansed. What Jesus may have feared was the very thing that has been tried again and again over the centuries: systematize the Christian movement, centralize it, and balloon it up in order to make an impression.

3. Denial of Risk and Peril

Collins' third stage of decline emerges when leaders and organizations ignore or minimize critical information, or refuse to listen to things they do not want to hear. The result is taking risks that are not properly assessed and that later take a serious bite out of organizational life. One of my favorite secondary Bible stories features the conversation between Kings Ahab and Jehoshaphat. The two meet to consider declaring war against Ramoth Gilead. A prudent Jehoshaphat says, "[Let's] first seek the counsel of the LORD."

Dutifully, Ahab rounds up four hundred prophets and solicits their opinion. The unanimous answer is that war is a smart decision. But Ahab had tilted the scales of opinion by bringing in false prophets.

Jehoshaphat, smelling a rat, asks, "Is there not a prophet of the LORD here of whom we can inquire?"

Ahab's answer is remarkable: "There is still one man through whom we can inquire of the LORD, but I hate him because he never prophesies anything good about me, but always bad. He is Micaiah . . ." (1 Kgs. 22:8).

When Micaiah arrives in the kings' presence, he acts exactly as Ahab expected. He outlines with clarity what would happen if Ahab and Jehoshaphat go to war. And he was right on the money. Ultimately, Ahab dies in the battle.

Collins worries about organizations who base their decisions on inadequate or mismanaged information. Perhaps he would worry even more about church congregations that don't even bother to gather data and rely instead on hearsay or impressions.

Early in my own leadership, I learned the danger of listening to comments that began, "They're saying . . ." or "The other day I heard . . ." or "Lots of people feel . . ." I grew to appreciate the unreliability of this "data."

The most valuable information came through trusted, wise people who were empowered to systematically engage the community in conversation, with questions designed ahead of time. This made it possible for the leadership team to assess the will, the faith, and the alignment of the people whenever we were testing the next steps in our organizational life. Of course, nothing was more useful to me than the information I gathered myself from face-to-face conversations with individuals and small groups.

4. Grasping for Salvation

The fourth stage begins, Collins writes, "when an organization reacts to a downturn by lurching for a silver bullet." He gives examples such as taking a huge risk on an unproven product, investing in an image makeover, hiring promise-making consultants, or seeking a new hero-type leader who can ride in on a white horse and single-handedly save the day.

When I tried to find biblical precedents for this principle, I was drawn to King Saul. Israel, desperate for a king so that they could be like other nations, picked the man because he came from a prominent family, had good looks, and was great with words. The people were delirious with the kind of optimism you see when a professional team acquires a superstar and is sure that they are now on the way to a championship.

In their own words: "We want a king over us. Then we will be like all the other nations, with a king to lead us and to go out before us and fight our battles" (1 Sam. 8:19). Sounds like a silver bullet to me. Sometimes silver bullets actually work, but as Jim Collins seems to be saying, probably not in most cases.

Silver-bullet Saul prospered for a short time, but the truth was that he didn't have the inner character to be the kind of leader that could build Israel into a stable kingdom and draw out its potential greatness. As the pressure rose, a hidden, more real Saul began to reveal himself until God simply withdrew his support. Saul's death on a battlefield where he was desperate for a victory is pathetic.

I remember times when I felt desperate for a breakthrough victory to stem the tide of what seemed to be a church sliding backward. Instead of examining how our congregation was doing in its fundamental practices of being servant-like people centered on the lordship of Christ, there was the temptation to go for the overnight revival, the special program, the high-performance staff member. I remember trying to write the perfect and passionate sermon that would realign everything overnight. Now I see this for what it was: the search for salvation in a gimmick, be it a presentation, a person, or a program.

Thankfully, I learned, as did those around me, that gimmicks almost never worked. Only when we went back to caring for people, discipling teachable leaders, introducing people to Jesus, and worshiping with a hearty spirit did things get back on track.

It all leads, Collins writes, to stage five . . .

5. Capitulation to Irrelevance or Death

If businesses run out of cash, organizations like churches run out of faith and spirit.

I think the temple in Jerusalem must have been nearly like that when Jesus walked out of it and said, "I'm not coming back." He was anticipating a day in the near future when the temple would be little more than a pile of stones.

Not long ago, I stood in front of a church building in Wales. A "For Sale" sign was tacked to the door. The cornerstone showed that it was built at the highwater mark of the Welsh revival. Now it is ensconced in weeds and clearly had been in a state of disuse for many years.

At what point did it start down the slope of organizational death? Who missed the hidden signs? Who ignored the core convictions? Who misinterpreted the information? Who went for the home-run ball, swung, and missed?

Great questions. Ignored, the mighty fall.

FOR FURTHER REFLECTION

1. *Have you been a part of an organization that is focused on growing larger and larger, losing sight of its soul? What have you done to prevent this?*

2. *In your opinion, why did Solomon have to set aside wisdom and pursue more and more material things? Can you think of a contemporary example of this?*

3. *In the organization(s) that you are a part of, are there some hidden signs that are perhaps being missed? Are any core convictions being overlooked? How can you address this?*

THE RIGHT WAY TO HANDLE CHURCH CONFLICT

We may say then, that the Jerusalem Council secured a
double victory—a victory of truth in confirming the Gospel
of grace, and a victory of love in preserving the fellowship by
sensitive concessions to conscientious Jewish scruples.

JOHN STOTT

I am by nature an idealist. I start almost everything in life by think-ing about the best-case scenario. As a young man, I had a best-case scenario for my marriage. As a father, I had the best-case scenario for raising our children. Being a pastor, I always think about the best pos-sibilities before anything else.

But when you're a person who is an idealist in most senses, you discover you have to live with disappointment, because nothing ever quite reaches the height of the ideal you create in your mind. Those of you who are like me can understand exactly what I'm saying. Those of you who are not like me might think this is silly. But disappointment can be a way of life for a lot of us.

A lot of us have an idealistic view of the church. We look at the New Testament, in particular the book of Acts, and we see a church that shook its world. We think how wonderful it would be to be part of that congregation. Everything just seems to have gone so right. Don't believe it—the New Testament church had some tough moments. And it's impressive that the Holy Spirit, inspiring the New Testament writers, didn't spare us from the grimy details. Sometimes the Holy Spirit shows us people at their worst.

One of my idealistic tendencies is to think the best about all possible communities. Over the years, I've had to learn that when you enter a marriage, you marry a sinner. And you shouldn't be surprised if you yourself, as a sinner, show a little sin on occasion as well.

It's the same thing being part of a church. When you are part of a church, there are times when you are going to see sin, when people are going to disappoint you. I've had to come to the realization that whenever two or more people get together and form a community, it will always be rather messy. When people get together, sooner or later the idealism will be blasted with a dose of reality. We struggle to communicate and understand. Because we are often innately selfish, messiness will often dictate the state of affairs.

Early Church Messiness

We see this vividly in Acts 15. To my thinking, this chapter contains one of the most important stories in all of the New Testament. This is an important story because it could have been the terminal point of the early church. All that wonderful stuff in the first fourteen chapters of Acts could have blown apart and been destroyed if the people of the Lord had not handled this moment correctly under the power of the Spirit.

Let me first offer a frame around the story, a backdrop. Acts 14:26 gives a summary about the ending of Paul and Barnabas' first missionary journey: "From Attalia they sailed back to Antioch, where they had been committed to the grace of God for the work they had now completed." That's an easy sentence to skip over, but it's worth pondering. Paul and Barnabas started this journey in chapter 13 with the call of the Holy Spirit. They went through tremendous challenges. We know as we study all the text relating to this first missionary journey that Paul had been stoned and left for dead. He had been deathly ill at one point. Paul and Barnabas had faced terrible slander, yet they had completed the trip. They had done the job completely; there were no loose ends, according to the call of the Spirit of God.

In Acts 14:27, we read that upon returning to Antioch, they went to their home church, the one that had dispatched and commissioned them. How glad they must have been to get home to familiar territory, to familiar cultures and customs and friends they dearly loved! And the welcome mat was out. When they arrived home, Paul and Barnabas gathered the church together and reported all that God had done through them—how he had opened a door of faith to the Gentiles. That was unprecedented. Before this moment, the people at Antioch had known only a few Gentiles here and there who had been saved. But now the church was getting reports of avalanches of Gentiles coming to faith. A revival, an awakening, was going on.

Think about the excitement those people in Antioch were experiencing. Think about how thrilled that crowd must have been as they listened to story after story of what God was doing. Think about the enthusiasm that filled that church. If you have been a Christ-follower for long, you are familiar with moments such as this when you get into one of those places where the Spirit of God is at work and lives are being transformed—you just get caught up in it.

Unfortunately, starting in Acts 15:1, the mood switches. "Certain people came down from Judea to Antioch and were teaching the believers, 'Unless you are circumcised, according to the custom taught by Moses, you cannot be saved.'"

How often have you had the experience of being on a roll, with something wonderful happening, and then into that moment comes somebody who throws a wet blanket on the whole thing? They look at what to you is obviously the blessing of the Lord, and they take it in a different direction, and somehow dull the whole thing. That's what happened in Antioch. In the midst of all this enthusiasm and excitement, some people came down from Jerusalem and cut across the grain of their joy. Paul and Barnabas said, "Something is wrong here."

The something wrong was this: These men maintained a Judaistic, Pharisaical perspective on Christian faith, which says that a person—particularly a Gentile—cannot be saved unless he is circumcised and upholds the entire law of Moses.

In today's society, we are a bit delicate about discussing the word circumcision and its meaning. In those days, however, people used the word with regularity and no embarrassment. We all know that in the Jewish tradition, the centuries-old covenant between God and the Jewish community had been that the male child was to be circumcised on the eighth day. This physical symbol reminded the people of the bond they had as people chosen of the Lord.

Conflict arises even among well-meaning people. We need to be fair to these men who went to Antioch. We need to cut them a bit of slack. They were believers too. But they had inherited a millennia-long tradition. They were wired to believe that a person could not be a child of God unless he upheld the law of Moses and unless he was circumcised. This was a no-brainer to these men: If the Gentiles were going to come into the church and be a part of the movement of the people of God—and that was a bothersome thought in itself—they would have to do it just as the Jewish men did it.

It's easy for me to look at this passage and think, *You guys are off the wall. This is stupid.* That's easy to think because I come from twenty centuries of New Testament Christian teaching in which circumcision is not a necessity for being a believer. While this may look dumb to me, it didn't look dumb to them.

That's an important learning experience for any of us who get into a situation where people resist change. I have to remind myself that there are people who seriously believe what they advocate, and before I disrespect them or turn my back on them, I need to understand where they are coming from.

These men had good intentions. Even so, they cast a wet blanket on the church's joy, and the church suddenly found itself in the beginnings of trouble. Acts 15:2 says, "This brought Paul and Barnabas into sharp dispute and debate with them." These aren't kind words. Don't launder those words and think this was just some quiet, polite conversation. These people were angry at each other. This church was suddenly in trouble. And its people could not handle this debate. It was getting out of control.

There are several examples of this kind of debate in the New Testament church. For example, at one point Paul wrote to the Philippians and said in effect, "Church, I beg you to bring Euodia and Syntyche [two leading women] together so they are of one mind and things won't get out of control."

Communities are messy. They look good on the surface, but they can have terrific struggles within. The church in Antioch looked good on the surface, but there was messiness beneath the surface. How would it be solved? You may think, *Why should I bother with a story that is more than nineteen hundred years old? What does it have to teach me?* I think you'll discover the church in Antioch has a lot to teach us by how they resolved conflict.

Churches *can* work through conflict. The Antioch church said, "Look, this is a bigger question than we can resolve." So in verse 3 we read that the church sent Paul and Barnabas and the other believers back to Jerusalem, to ask the mother church to resolve this conflict.

Acts 15:3–4 states: "As they traveled through Phoenicia and Samaria, they told how the Gentiles had been converted. This news made all the believers very glad. When they came to Jerusalem, they were welcomed by the church and the apostles and elders, to whom they reported everything God had done through them."

But when the reports were given, the dispute took on a new flame. Some of the believers who belonged to the party of the Pharisees—Christian Pharisees—stood and reiterated the argument: "The Gentiles must be circumcised and required to keep the law of Moses." In other words, "If these folks from outside are going to come and be a part of our movement, they have to do it exactly as we did it." These were good people, deserving of our respect, and they were speaking out of a tradition that was hundreds and hundreds of years old.

And so, the church meeting began. If this meeting had not gone well, it probably would have divided and paralyzed (or at least neutralized) the movement of early Christ-followers, and the church as we have known it through the centuries would never have happened.

I believe this is a more significant moment than even the Lutheran Reformation. This situation paints a picture of how Christians were at cross-purposes with each other, had a disagreement, and handled it well. We've seen other situations through Church history when Christians mishandled their disagreements, and the next generations paid a terrible price.

Solving the Dispute

The story continues to unfold in Acts 15:6. "The apostles and elders met to consider this question." What happened in this meeting, as Luke records, were many speeches, and the meeting probably lasted several days. All we have, though, are a few compressed excerpts from at least three speeches.

The first speech came from the apostle Peter. He said: "Brothers, you know that some time ago God made a choice among you that the Gentiles might hear from my lips the message of the Gospel and believe. God, who knows the heart, showed that he accepted them by giving the Holy Spirit to them, just as he did to us" (vv. 7–8). Peter was alluding, of course, to the conversion of Cornelius in Acts 10.

And Peter at that point learned and accepted what every Jewish Christian was struggling to get used to: that a Gentile could be saved and filled with the Spirit. Everyone thought in those days that only Jews could be saved. This seems ridiculous to modern Christians, yet this was deadly serious to first-century Jews.

The basic point Peter was trying to make was that the believers needed to understand that God was doing a great work, that he accepted the Gentiles just as he accepts the Jews. Look at what was going on out through southern Turkey and Syria where Paul and Barnabas had been doing their missionary work.

By the way, if you go to the second chapter of Galatians, you will discover that this speech was not easy for Peter to make. When he was in Antioch, he was waffling on this same issue. Peter didn't change easily. Paul says in Galatians 2:11 that he had to rebuke Peter in front of the entire church. We wouldn't do that today, but Paul did. Right in front of everybody, Paul opposed him to his face, saying, "Peter, you're wrong."

Peter had been eating with Gentiles for a while until some of his Jewish friends came, and then he restricted himself to eating only with

Jews. Paul told him in no uncertain terms that he was a hypocrite. But Peter finally had the humility to admit that Paul was right.

That's why Peter is able to get up in front of the Jerusalem Council and say: "[God] did not discriminate between us and them, for he purified their hearts by faith. Now then, why do you try to test God by putting on the necks of Gentiles a yoke that neither we nor our ancestors have been able to bear?" (Acts 15:9–10). When Peter finished, the whole assembly became silent as they listened to Barnabas and Paul.

A Lack of Listening

One of the problems I see in our modern generation is that we often don't do a good job of listening to each other. We hold our positions hard and fast, whether on economics or politics or theology. Many of us enter discussions thinking, *I know what's right, and it doesn't make any difference what you think.* We are becoming brittle and rigid, which is infiltrating the church and beyond it, wherever you look. As a society, we have to learn to be silent, just as the congregation in this passage was. We have to listen and try to perceive where the voice of God is speaking in the midst of life today.

Back in Jerusalem, the leaders sat silently, listening to Barnabas and Paul talk about the miraculous signs and wonders God had done through them to the Gentiles. When Paul and Barnabas finished, James spoke up. Somehow, without any explanation, James had risen to the surface to be the leader, the spokesperson of the church. James said, "Brothers, listen to me. Simon has described to us how God first intervened to choose a people for his name from the Gentiles. The words of the prophets are in agreement with this" (Acts 15:13–15). Then he quoted the prophet Amos, who predicted centuries before that Gentiles would become part of the people of God.

In verse 19, James boldly asserts his judgment on the matter. He did not say, "Let's vote on it." Instead, James said, "It is my judgment," and he pronounced one of the most serious theological conclusions the church has ever known in its two thousand years of history.

"It is my judgment, therefore, that we should not make it difficult for the Gentiles who are turning to God." James was saying, "We've got a whole world out there to win, and we've got to do our best to make sure that people outside the pale of the cross, who are different than we are, are made to feel as welcome as possible. While we're going to adhere to the key convictions of the Gospel, we are not going to add one scintilla more to it than is necessary, so people will feel welcomed whether they are Jews or Gentiles."

Today, we would do well to memorize verse 19. In too many places today, the church is making it harder and harder for people outside the faith to hear the Gospel. We don't mean to do it, but we make it difficult for the young to make commitments. We make it difficult for the person who has a postmodern mind to hear the Gospel.

James proposes that they write a letter (vv. 24–28):

We have heard that some went out from us without our authorization and disturbed you, troubling your minds by what they said. So we all agreed to choose some men and send them to you with our dear friends Barnabas and Paul—men who have risked their lives for the name of our Lord Jesus Christ. . . . It seemed good to the Holy Spirit and to us not to burden you with anything beyond the following requirements.

In other words, the letter said: "Here are two or three things we would appreciate you Gentiles considering. Circumcision is not necessary. But we wish you would normally abstain from doing some things that are terribly offensive to our Jewish brothers."

The law of love was in motion here. They were making a compromise. While they weren't asking the Gentile men to be circumcised, they were asking them, out of respect for their Jewish spiritual forefathers, to refrain from doing some things the Jews have considered over the centuries to be important. It was another way of saying, "Don't needlessly offend the Jews, but find your freedom in Christ and go on as Paul and Barnabas have instructed you."

Notice, by the way, when the letter was written, it was hand-delivered. It wasn't a letter from the email culture. And even today, sometimes words need a face. The Jerusalem church sent the letter with some godly men so the congregations out there would hear the gentleness, firmness, conviction, and holiness behind how this decision was made.

Two Key Lessons

What can we learn from this story? *First, the church in Jerusalem made sure that the essence, the core conviction of the Gospel, was never compromised.* Throughout this debate, the cross of Christ, the blood of the Lord shed for our sins, and the call to repentance, were never compromised. The church understood what people—whether Jew or Gentile—have to do to be powerfully saved.

This might have been a moment when the Gospel of salvation could have been terribly confused, and the church could have divided over doctrinal misunderstandings and splits. But the church preserved what Paul would say in 1 Corinthians 1, when he said that if anyone removes the cross from the Gospel in any way, shape, or form, they're wrong. And thus, the Gospel of salvation was preserved in this great debate.

Second, they preserved the unity of the body of Christ. No one walked. This is not always true in today's society. We are being so acculturated by a customized society in which every person wants everything his or her way. Whether we're talking about business, clothing, or our jobs, we increasingly expect that it's done our way. If not, we walk. You often see that attitude in the church today—*Do it my way, or I walk.*

The beauty of this chapter in Acts is that people disagreed with each other sharply, but they preserved the integrity and the unity of the body. I'm sure not everybody left that meeting happy. Some people must have been profoundly disturbed, but they hung in there. The church and its mission went forward because the Spirit of God spoke.

This is a powerful story of how people act when communities are messy. Even though good people see things in different ways, the Gospel is integral and the unity is preserved. That's the way conflict should be handled.

FOR FURTHER REFLECTION

1. *Think of a time when circumstances or people caused you to feel disappointed. What was the emotional impact of that disappointment in your life?*

2. *Think of a time when a group you were a part of was harmonious and cohesive and then became split over a difference of opinion. How was the issue resolved? How did you feel about what happened, and what part did you play in things?*

3. *In business or church situations, how can you as a leader not compromise key essentials while still preserving a sense of unity and harmony?*

SOMETIMES YOU JUST NEED TO DISAPPEAR

Every now and then go away, have a little
relaxation, for when you come back to your
work your judgment will be surer.

LEONARDO DA VINCI

I often think of an innkeeper Gail and I met in Vermont. Everything about him seemed unusual: his dress, his use of language, the ambience of his inn. He aroused my curiosity, and I began asking questions. I learned that Jack Coleman had been the president of Haverford, a well-known college in Pennsylvania. Later, he had become the head of a prestigious educational foundation. Now in semiretirement, he ran an inn. I also learned that he had acquired the lifelong habit of regularly disappearing for short periods of time. He simply dropped out of sight. Presumably some assistant (or relative) knew where to find him, but the rest of the people in his world didn't.

When he resurfaced (usually about ten days later), he would tell how he'd worked as a shoe-shine man at a railroad station or as part of a garbage collection team. Once he bussed tables at a fast-food restaurant. *Why?*

"Because," he said, "in my line of executive work, it's easy to lose touch with the larger, very real world of common people. And once a leader loses that touch, a growing ineffectiveness seeps in. You forget where the real action of life is centered."

When I was just beginning in ministry, I spent about six months traveling every weekend to churches where I would lead seminars on creative forms of evangelism. The economics of the time forced me to stay in the homes of church members. Men (in particular) would talk with me in great candor about their attitudes toward faith and the church. Frequently, coffee in hand, their after-dinner conversation would turn to their pastor.

"We love our pastor," I would hear. "But if the truth be told, he has almost no comprehension of what life looks like for me from Monday to Friday. It shows in his sermons and in what he asks of people."

One man told me, "Our pastor reveals his view of our world in his Sunday benediction. He says, 'Lord, dismiss us with your blessing, and bring us back for prayer meeting on Wednesday. Be with the youth on their retreat next Friday night. Help us to get more Sunday school teachers. Amen.'" My host went on, "My pastor doesn't seem to know that I have a job; his perspective is entirely church-centric."

I'm grateful for those weekend chats almost forty years ago. They changed the way I pastored. They convinced me that ministry is (brace yourself!) not about the church but about equipping and encouraging people for life during the week—in the home, in the marketplace, at school.

Years later, a church member said to me, "I know you eat, sleep, and drink this church every day of the week—and so you should. But you need to know that when I leave here, I may go for several days and not think about the church once. I'm too busy keeping up with my work, my family, and the pressures of life." He reminded me that I dare not assume everyone is as preoccupied with the church as I am.

What if pastors—at least those responsible for preaching and inseminating minds and hearts with fresh ideas about how to follow Jesus—occasionally disappeared like my college president friend? What would we learn?

Untested Holiness

Among my favorite stories is one—a couple of centuries old—that comes from eastern Europe.

A brilliant young Jewish scholar approached a wizened rabbi and asked, "They say I am the holiest of all men. Do you think this is true?" At first, the rabbi refused to answer. But after being badgered by the tenacious scholar, he responded, "You are the most pious man of our age. You study night and day, retired from the world, surrounded by the rows of your books, the holy ark, the faces of devout scholars. You have reached high holiness. But how have you reached it? Go down in the marketplace with the rest of the Jews. Endure their work, their strains, their distractions. Mingle in the world, hear the skepticism and irreligion they hear, take the blows they take. Let us see then if you remain the holiest of all men."

In my years as a pastor, I struggled with this. The very nature of the organization insisted on sucking me into its center, into conversations that centered on programs and problems, but rarely about ideas or the hands-on issues of weekday life. Almost no one ever said, "Go down to the marketplace! Disappear!" Even the boards to whom I was accountable saw little value in my getting away from my desk and its administrative demands.

If they had, I tell you, my sermons would have taken on far more color, far more useful application, far more realism. Maybe my leadership would have been a more mature kind.

What I did do to fight the system was this: I made it my goal to visit every church leader (and beyond when possible) where he or she worked. I filled my calendar with breakfasts and lunches near where people pursued their livelihood. Often I was invited to visit offices, construction sites, sales locations, and laboratories, where I met bosses, colleagues, and assistants.

But most importantly, I engaged people at their point of competence. They saw *me* at my best on Sunday; why shouldn't I see *them* where they enjoyed the home-field advantage?

Virtually every relationship changed for the better after such visits. In those encounters, I gained much of my sermon illustrations and more than a few ideas for sermons themselves. But most of all, there was a new credibility in the pastoral relationship.

I like to think Jesus ran his mission similarly. The Gospels do not record much of his work being done on religious campuses. He engaged people almost exclusively where they worked and traded, where they suffered and survived. His metaphors and stories appear to be drawn right from the context where he spoke. "A sower went out to sow . . . a woman was sweeping her floor . . . a man was settling his accounts." Those are the stories of someone who's been there.

I sometimes fear that recent pastoral ministry has taken a turn that could have long-range downsides. Pastors now have classy offices to which people come, having made appointments. And the common people rarely make it through the door. Email communication grows more prevalent.

In addition, pastors are often hired as preachers and evaluated as managers of programs. This involves numerous meetings, planning sessions, and budget appropriations—which means becoming separated from the common pastoral exposures that maximize people contact and spiritual (not administrative) effectiveness.

I know, because I've often fallen into those same traps. Too often I let the system control my priorities. I lapsed into believing that "org-talk" is more important than personal engagement out there.

Real-World Strategy

Nehemiah was once advised by "friends" to close himself inside the rebuilt temple so that his enemies could not get to him. However, the man was smart enough to recognize that his place was among the workers at the walls where the arrows were flying, not in the artificial world of the institution.

How can you fight this institutionalizing system? When I was in fighting form, I followed these general principles:

Book Real-World Appointments. I tried to book at least four or five meetings a week with people in the congregation that were not about problems or programs but rather about "life in the real world" and how it could be more powerfully shaped by the influence of Jesus. I tried to schedule these meetings near or at the places where these people worked.

Ask Stretching Questions. I did my best to focus conversation on the things most pressing in the lives of others rather than on myself. I tried to ask creative questions about their dreams, their fears, their greatest challenges. I asked about their families (if married), or their friends (if single). If time permitted, I asked what they needed as participants in our church community—not what I had to "sell" them. The best compliment I could receive was, "Gee, you ask great questions. No one has ever asked me that before."

Remember Key Events. Whenever possible, I noted in my calendar events and deadlines that people were facing in their work. I tried to send a card at the appropriate time, assuring them of my prayers at that moment. And I tried to follow up to learn what had happened.

Expand and Share My Reading. Even now, I try to expand the bandwidth of my reading to subject matter that acquaints me with the challenges facing the people to whom I preach each week. When possible, I send copies of book chapters or articles to people when I think it would encourage them.

Practice Workplace Prayer. I always tried to pray for these people in the context of their work. "Lord, I ask you to fill this office with a powerful sense of your presence as my friend works . . ."; "Father, when anyone crosses the path of my friend today, I ask that the love of Christ will be . . ."; "Spirit of God, give my friend wisdom as he faces these work issues this afternoon."

Use Marketplace Language. I still try to incorporate real-world language into my preaching. "You use too many business terms in your preaching," I hear occasionally. And it's possible that I overdo it. But I note that Paul's writings are jammed with business terms, athletic analogies, and military references. He was in the middle of it all!

Lessons from the Pit Crew

My grandson Lucas and I recently sat down to watch a NASCAR race on television. He loves speed; I love teamwork. I was fascinated with the work of the pit crews. Did you know that a good pit crew can change four tires, fill the gas tank, wipe off the windshield, and give the driver a drink (and maybe even replace a fender) in 15.8 seconds? A *good* pit-crew, I said!

Their goal? To get the driver and the car—fully operational—back into the race. Because the race is what it's all about. Races are lost if one spends too much time in the pit.

Do our churches know this? Do I? Imagine a crew standing around when the driver needs a push back into the racing lanes. What happens if the pit crew forgets that the action is out there and not (apart from 15.8 seconds) in the pit? When I watch a pit crew working together to get the driver's car prepared, I see a vision of pastors and associates: fueling, fixing, and pushing the people back into the race.

The Real-Life Race

As a pastor, I became convinced of the importance of the benediction at the end of the service as a way of reminding people that they were headed back to the "race" of real life. I would offer this benediction to them as I lifted my hands and made the sign of the cross over them:

Go forth into the streets of this world. Go with the memory of this hour when you have refreshed your souls in the presence of God and his people. Go with the intention to be faithful to Jesus. Go with the promise that you will carry his love and extend it to your family and your friends, to those whom you meet along the way who are in need. Go with courage, with a resolve not to sin, and go with the exciting reminder that at any moment, Jesus may come again. In the name of the Father, Son, and Holy Spirit, I bid you farewell.

FOR FURTHER REFLECTION

1. *How often do you remove yourself from your day-to-day activities in order to connect with "real life"? Where have you chosen to go in order to understand what those in your congregation face on a daily basis?*

2. *Name some positive results that stem from immersing yourself in the lives and interests of those you serve.*

3. *What are some key ways you've developed to relate to the individuals in your congregation, not just spiritually but as human beings?*

TEN CONDITIONS FOR CHURCH GROWTH

*Church growth comes out of church health. Focusing on
growth alone misses the point. When congregations are
healthy, they grow the way God intends. Healthy churches
don't need gimmicks to grow—they grow naturally.*

RICK WARREN

Why do churches grow? In the midst of all the conferences, seminars,
and books on the subject, I sense that Christian leaders are overlooking
some very important matters. If we continue to ignore certain indispensable conditions, the result may be a short-range, artificial church growth
that will explode like a tense bubble. To achieve long-range, real church
growth, we must grapple with those underpinning aspects of church life
that allow the people of God to outlive any one personality or method.

The conditions I am about to enumerate always surface as matters of
discussion and crisis when a church approaches certain growth plateaus.
Another term for these plateaus might be "growth ceilings"—points at
which a church ceases to grow any further without some major effort.

Often a church appears to pause numerically as if it were wrestling with the practicality and desirability of breaking through to the next growth level. This period of congregational doldrums is often characterized by depressing board meetings and quiet conversations in homes and church hallways about "What's gone wrong with our church?" or "I can remember when everything seemed to be going so well, and we were growing every week."

What is really happening, however, is that the church is facing into whether it has the faith and energy to break through a natural growth ceiling. Many churches fail to take the steps needed, and they flatten out at that plateau. Later, they may move into a state of slow decline both in numbers and vitality.

The first plateau is when a congregation reaches a regular attendance of 150 in its major services. A second plateau is attained at 450 to 500. Still a third appears somewhere in the range of 950 to 1000.

There seem to be some practical reasons for these three plateaus, and at each level they appear to be quite similar. Only the magnitude is different. To break through a ceiling demands certain decisions on the part of a congregation. Usually those decisions revolve around more building space, additional pastoral staffing, and a subconscious willingness to allow more people into the church fellowship than any one person will ever be able to know personally. Any one or a combination of these three things tends to threaten the best of us as church members, and our quiet reluctance to spend more money, relinquish control, or associate with virtual "strangers" makes us uneasy.

The tendency, therefore, is to put off dramatic decisions. Often, as a result, the decisions are made anyway, for not to decide is actually to decide to stagnate. Overcrowded space, overloaded pastors, and people reluctant to form new relationships will kill a church faster than anything else.

Having broken through a plateau or ceiling, a church usually begins a steady growth trend toward the next ceiling. There the same kind of trauma sets in again until people feel certain of themselves and God's leading. It appears that once a church makes bold enough decisions to break through the third successive ceiling, unlimited growth tends to happen in regular phases.

I am convinced that a large majority of the following conditions must be in force within a congregation, or whatever growth there is will be forced and probably temporary. To be sure, a church can grow on the singular strength of a charismatic personality, or a local situation in which there is an influx into the community, or a kind of momentary programming fad. But is this the kind of growth we desire? Certainly not! We seek honest, long-range growth in which disciples are being shaped in the image of Jesus Christ.

Condition 1: Building for Growth

A growing congregation has somehow made a decision that it will project a ministry to its people built on the future, not focused on the present. This means that it builds structures, hires pastoral staff, and sets in motion programs based on anticipated growth, not actual growth.

To program on the basis of actual growth is always to be at least one to two years behind the momentum. Unfortunately, most churches wait, for example, to hire a youth minister until the youth have arrived, perhaps growing up through the ranks of preschool and children's departments. Suddenly the leadership panics, realizing it needs more professional ministry for its young people. But where to find someone? That may be a six-month project, followed by four months of acclimating the person to the staff, followed by six to nine months of stabilization. Too much time has been lost for effective work.

The same, obviously, could be said about buildings and programs. Building for growth in terms of staff, space, and strategy is an act of faith. But as in the miracle of the fishes, Jesus fills only those nets that are out of the boat and in the water. A church wishing to grow builds space, staff, and strategy today for tomorrow's needs.

Condition 2: Structural Renewal

When a jet plane crashes through the sound barrier, it sets up an aerodynamic tension. Engineers tell me they must design an airplane for this possibility. Many churches are based on a constitutional and programmatic structure put together when they were one-fifth their present size. They wonder why growth is not taking place, and the answer may lie in the fact that yesterday's configuration makes them incapable of crashing through the growth barriers. A larger church requires centralized policy making but decentralized policy implementation.

Unwilling to share the responsibility for significant ministry, a small group at the top can seriously entangle a church's capacity to conform to change. John Gardner, in an article on organizational renewal, said that a growing organization reviews its constitutional and strategic structure annually with an eye to changing virtually anything that limits its growth and efficiency.

Today, a church should be willing to change anything except its doctrinal distinctives. It should be prepared to discontinue any program the minute it does not reach its expected potential. And it should be prepared to put into action anything wise leaders feel can work to achieve biblical objectives for the health of the believers.

Condition 3: Subcongregations

The instant a church pushes through a ceiling of 150, it consists of at least two or more subcongregations. These are groups with an affinity: geographical location, similar tasks within the church structure, or shared similarities of age, education, or professional interests.

The choir of a church can be a subcongregation. Sunday school teachers, youth staff workers, and the evangelistic calling team are subcongregations. So is the young married group and the senior adult class. The point is this: the larger a church becomes, the more subcongregations will appear. They are the basis of fellowship for each believer. When someone says, "The church is getting so large I don't know everyone," the answer is simple: "No one has to know everyone; just make sure you are a member of a subcongregation. No one can relate to more than forty or fifty people anyway, and the subcongregational structure allows for relationships within a large church." The Jerusalem church was obviously a large church, and its subcongregations met "from house to house."

With subcongregations, the size of a church becomes irrelevant. The old debate about the virtues of small churches and large churches is quite meaningless. Our attention ought to center on whether or not there are subcongregational groups to which anyone can attach himself.

Condition 4: Diversified Staffing

Growing churches must give serious attention to the multiple-staff concept. Many churches wait far too long to implement this. Only after the pastor has begged and cajoled, only after he has worked himself into exhaustion, is the congregation willing to respond.

A good formula for multiple staffing is this: In addition to a senior pastor, a staff pastor of some kind must be appointed for every two hundred regularly attending persons. Staff pastors offer a church specialized styles of ministry: youth, children, music, administration. Usually a church responds to the most critical need on the surface. Youth ministry is one example. The greater hidden need in many churches may be in the area of administrative coordination. A sensitive and prayerful leadership will—in conjunction with the pastor—determine the need for staff and build a staff well ahead of the panic moment.

Five small churches must each have a preaching minister who does everything else required of a pastor. One large church can employ five specialized pastors, each providing a special kind of service to a large segment of the church family. This fact should not be easily overlooked; it makes a big difference in confronting the many needs today.

Condition 5: Pursuit of Excellence

As a church grows larger, it needs to make sure that participants in major services sing, read, and lead at the highest possible caliber. Allowing unqualified people to carry out leadership functions simply because "everyone ought to have a chance" cannot work in a large church. If reasonable excellence cannot be achieved, the person in question should be exposed to other opportunities in which his or her gifts can be better used and appreciated.

The question of excellence is frequently confused with Hollywoodism. I am aware that I shall never convince all the skeptics on this one, but the fact is that a growing church has newcomers each week who are making long-range decisions on first impressions. They are confronted with excellence every day of the week in entertainment, business, and community. The work of God cannot be represented by anything less than the standard to which the culture is accustomed. Shabbiness in preaching, music, administration, and programming will quench a growing church's momentum very quickly.

Condition 6: Systematic Pulpit Ministry

Long-term real church growth rests heavily on a systematic ministry of preaching that feeds people. Basically, this is a ministry that comes from *one* preacher. Over a long period of time, it cannot be shared by a team of preachers (although there are a few unusual experiments across the country that speak to the contrary). I am convinced that most American churches demand a one-man pulpit ministry that systematically teaches the Word of God.

Churches can grow for a period of time on the basis of attractive programs; they can momentarily benefit from the work of specialists being flown in for special functions. But long-term growth depends upon whether or not the senior minister can preach well enough to feed the inner spirits of worshipers.

The preaching must be biblical in base, applicable to life, and confrontational in terms of requiring a constant series of decisions about personal living standards and relationships. People need to know how they should live and how they should cope with the pressures crushing down upon them each week. Where there is a pulpit giving honest answers to real-life questions based on exposition from God's Word, there will be growth.

Condition 7: Full-Spectrum Education

Growth in numbers must be accompanied with total commitment to church education. This is not just Sunday school, although it begins there. And it is not education targeted only at children, although it includes them. It is education aimed at every human being in the church, from four-week-old infants who are brought to a warmly lit and comfortable nursery to gain their first impressions of church to the most aged member sitting in a class on Bible exposition.

Full-spectrum education includes classes and learning experiences for new as well as mature Christians. It provides a curriculum in which all parts of the Bible and Christian doctrine are examined. And it offers practical courses on ethics and ideas, where Christianity challenges the modern worldview.

Full-spectrum education implies not only a massive effort toward good teaching, but it demands that no reasonable costs be avoided to provide the most comfortable and effective learning facilities. Long-term real growth cannot happen without everyone involved in Christian education.

Condition 8: Disciplined Membership

When I speak of a disciplined membership, I am talking about at least two things: membership that is not cheap, and membership that compels involvement.

A growing church sets high standards for anyone wishing to identify with the church family. It makes every wise effort to ascertain a person's personal relationship to God and God's people. It tests integrity through interviews, classes, and confrontations with the needs of the church. Short-term artificial growth can be achieved by making membership a simple matter, but long-term growth cannot happen unless the quality of members is ensured.

An involved membership is also part of discipline. Members should be expected to contribute at least four things: their loyalty to the major services of the church, their willingness to use their spiritual gifts when called upon, their financial gifts on a proportionate basis to God's blessing in their lives, and their positive and encouraging support of church leaders. Growth cannot happen without this.

Condition 9: Relational Emphasis

No church that is relationally cold will grow for very long. This condition begins with the pastor, who must show a sincere and honest love for people. If he is genuine in his love and capable of expressing it, the effect will be contagious. In a world that tends to exploit and dominate, people crave love. When they find it in a church fellowship, they wish to be part of it.

Warmth can be easily engendered in a large congregation as well as in a small one. But it begins with the leadership. The relational emphasis must pervade the church program, emphasizing the family structure and meaningful friendships that support people in times of need.

Growing churches must find ways to break people down into small, caring groups—perhaps different from subcongregations—where immediate attention can be given when a person faces a need caused by sickness, death, or professional difficulty. With such a relational emphasis, no one will ever feel lost, unneeded, or unloved. Growth demands it.

Condition 10: Bold Decisions

Church growth is ultimately accomplished in a climate of faith. No church is ever blessed by God's Spirit if it restricts its decision making to the obvious and the "safe." Faith demands a willingness to take large risks (which aren't really risks at all). As the disciples put nets into a sea seemingly bereft of fish, so the church is called upon by God to make bold moves to which God can respond with power and approval.

Bold decisions are not stupid ones. They are not the result of one person who wishes to build an organizational monument to himself. Rather, they are the believing decisions made by a prayerful leadership team of men and women of faith who are trusting God for great things. Bold decisions are made by people who are not totally sure of the results, but they know that their church belongs to the Lord and that where he leads it will be his concern. They step forth in faith, and God responds.

Where these conditions prevail, the plateaus of growth are easily passed. The church grows more significant to all of us as society becomes more anti-Christ. We cannot wait another moment; we must bring these conditions to pass so that more might hear, more might be won to Jesus Christ, and churches everywhere might grow.

FOR FURTHER REFLECTION

1. Think about the churches you've been a part of. Were you involved in a church growing from 150 to 500 members? 500 to 1000 or more? What role did you play in this growth?

2. What challenges have you encountered in small congregations? How about medium-sized congregations and larger? Do these challenges correlate to the size of the congregation, or are the challenges similar no matter what the size?

3. In your own words, what are the keys to healthy church growth?

MINISTRY'S SWEET SPOT

The methods that Jesus used to prepare his disciples
are an inspiring model for training and equipping
leaders and lay people for service. . . . Church is not
a place where people go but something that people
are, and understanding and utilizing one's gifts and
talents enrich both the body and the believer.

D. STUART BRISCOE

Recalling my early years in Christian ministry, I am embarrassed to realize how much I invested in something that could have been called "Gordon MacDonald, Inc." It was too much about me and not enough about Jesus and others.

Somewhere along the line, my self-building activities gave way to building an organization, a church organization. That meant recruiting teams, encouraging leaders, conceiving strategies that would cause a congregation to grow (both spiritually and numerically). Pastoring became a very satisfying experience, and I loved my work . . . most of the time.

But one weekend, after years of organization building, I awakened to something much better—a sweet spot of ministry, you could say, where it all just seemed right. Rather than building me or even building an organization, I discovered people-building, a ministry with younger Christians who—properly prepared—might go on to be difference-makers in some part of the kingdom.

That awakening happened when I visited the United States Military Academy at West Point as a speaker in the cadet chapel. I was astonished at the dignity and excellence of the men and women I met. It was unforgettable.

The mission of the USMA is:

To educate, train, and inspire the Corps of Cadets so that each graduate is a commissioned leader of character committed to the values of Duty, Honor, Country, and prepared for a career of professional excellence and service to the Nation as an officer in the United States Army.

This got me wondering: *What is the equivalent in the church where I pastor? Where and how do we educate, train, and inspire leaders capable of influencing others for the sake of Jesus Christ?* The truth was that we weren't doing that.

Oh, sure, we had leadership training among our programs. Our bulletin might read: "Anyone wanting training in this or that activity should come out on Wednesday night." In ninety minutes, we implied, we'll make you a leader. Kind of like the TV deals: three payments of $39.95, and we'll make you a real estate tycoon.

We wanted "players" who were unafraid to mix it up, experiment with ideas, and move the conversation along. That's not how it's done at West Point or Annapolis or the Air Force Academy. In those schools, it's not so simple.

New Leaders Don't Just Happen

When I returned home, I tried to sell my vision of a "West Point" leadership development effort to our staff, our lay leadership, to anyone willing to listen. Apparently I did a poor job. I got smiles, agreement in principle, and comments like, "We need to think about that . . . sometime." Admittedly, at first, I was all words and few specifics.

Then one day, I got it. A vision with no precedent in a church usually requires that someone (me, in this case) do the job himself.

A breakthrough occurred when my wife, Gail, realizing I was serious, said, "This is something you and I could do together. And I think we would be smart if we took the idea out of the church building and into our home." It was the first of her many bright ideas regarding this endeavor.

We searched for materials that fit our vision, and we found nothing satisfying. We realized that leadership development is not a program. It is about strong relationships in which people grow to be what God designed them to be. It's sort of like what Jesus made happen when he selected twelve learners to be with him. Twelve guys in whom he—and he only—saw leadership (or influence) potential.

Gail and I decided to select twelve to fourteen people and see what might be possible. One of my staff associates had been meeting with a small group of young adults. When he resigned to move to another ministry, I sat down with his group, told them about my dream, and asked if they would meet with Gail and me at our home a week later. They all agreed.

When the evening came, Gail and I shared the dream in detail. We proposed meeting weekly on Wednesday nights for about nine months.

"We'll try to tell you everything we've learned about following Jesus, hearing his call, discovering our individual giftedness, and what it means to grow in biblically defined character," we said. "We'll tell you whatever we've learned about influencing people.

"But here's the fine print," we said. "You will have to strip your calendar for about forty Wednesday nights so that you are here—on time, staying the full duration, fully prepared—every night. You can't miss unless you're dying or your company sends you out of town and tells you that you'll lose your job if you don't go."

We ended that first evening by telling the group, "Pray and think about this, and if you believe that God is leading you into this experience, call us." Within a few days, everyone called with his or her yes, and the schedule was set.

That was over ten years ago. And almost every year since, we have selected and launched a similar group. Today, Gail and I can identify about one hundred people who have gone through iterations of "West Point" and—almost without exception—are engaged in some significant effort in serving God. Several have gained degrees and are in formal ministry positions. The majority are exercising various forms of lay influence either inside their churches or in the larger world, doing good in the name of Jesus.

What We Do

Whenever I talk about this, people zoom in. They want to know more. They realize the importance of this for a church's long-term future. How do you train tomorrow's Christian leaders?

We called our efforts LDI: Leadership/Discipleship Initiative. I don't remember exactly why, except West Point wasn't quite to everyone's liking.

"Do you have a curriculum?" I am often asked.

The answer is that there is no $39.95 curriculum. I wonder if Jesus had a curriculum to follow up his words, "Follow me . . ." In the nineteenth century, an Englishman, A. B. Bruce, wrote a book, *The Training of the Twelve,* in which he tried to trace the curriculum Jesus followed. I highly recommend his book, but I warn you: It's no easy read.

LDI is an intuitive approach to leadership development. Gail and I knew the outcomes we wanted, and we knew some of the disciplines we wanted to teach. What we didn't know was how it would flow from week to week.

Now, over ten years later, we are able to describe what we have done and what we have learned. Our goals for each group were:

- To identify people with potential to influence others if they were appropriately coached.

- To accelerate their spiritual growth so that they would become strong, self-nourishing followers of Jesus who would seek to grow in godliness for the rest of their lives.

- To give them an experience of all that the Christian community is capable of becoming when people truly love one another as Jesus loves us.

- To demonstrate what it means to feel called and gifted, and to discover that there is no greater joy than to be caught up in God's purposes for a particular generation.

We suspected that if we simply put an ad in the church bulletin, saying, in effect, "Come to Gail and Gordon's house on Wednesday nights, and we'll teach you how to be leaders," we would be inundated, and a large percentage would come for the wrong reasons.

It has often been noted that Jesus tended to be unreceptive to volunteers. Believing that to be a significant principle, we decided to make LDI something different from anything else in the church. We would vet people, quietly and discreetly.

As that first LDI year came to an end, Gail and I began to search for our next "dozen." We commenced our search early in February because the September start date was only eight months away.

As we drove home from various church activities, our conversations often focused on the people we were observing. Since Gail is particularly good at studying people and making intuitive judgments, I relied heavily upon her insights.

"I was watching Bob this morning," she'd say. Or, "Have you ever thought about Craig and Lori . . ." And we'd talk about what we were both seeing.

Did they show evidences of faithfulness, of spiritual desire, of seeking ways to serve? We were not going to invite people into LDI who had not shown they were loyal to their commitments and covenants. Many church folk are good with their words and promises, but quickly fold when the excitement of something new morphs into something that is more or less routine. Faithfulness to us began with a reputation for showing up (on time, prepared, and generally enthusiastic).

We were not interested in people who got attention by having chronic problems. LDI was not meant to be a support or therapy group. There is a place for such gatherings in the congregation, but LDI wasn't one of them.

Yes, LDI people have struggles during the year. Who doesn't? Someone loses a job, a spouse becomes seriously ill, a son or daughter presents a worrisome problem. Under those circumstances, the LDI groups experienced the joy of coming alongside each other: praying, caring, and serving one another. We all learned how to "pastor" and how to pray for each other.

What We Looked For

In short, we were looking for:

- *People who were teachable.* Individuals who asked good questions, who took seriously the Christ-following life, who went out of their way to grow spiritually.

- *People with essential social skills.* People who showed respect and regard for others, not so argumentative or abrasive or touchy that they didn't fit well with others.

- *People who would not simply sit for an entire evening saying nothing.* We wanted "players" who were unafraid to mix it up, experiment with ideas, move the conversation along, and venture opinions.

By May or June, we usually had a list of twenty people that we had observed, prayed over, even quietly tested a bit (without their realizing it). In August or early September, we would invite them all to our home for dinner.

After dessert, we would gather the group and tell them the story of how the LDI idea evolved. We would share our objectives and some of the things we believed God had done in previous groups. We would recount stories of various participants who were now in some form of leadership (with their permission, of course) and assure our guests that they could go to any of these former LDIers and ask them about their experience.

It was important during the evening to tell everyone what we had seen in them and why we felt led to invite them. This turned out to be significant. For many, this was the first time they had ever had anyone identify characteristics in them that marked them as potential influencers.

Before the evening ended, we came to the "ask."

We're inviting each of you to consider LDI for the next year. But we don't want you to accept our invitation until you've spent several days thinking through the implications. It's going to mean every Wednesday night (later this became Monday night) for about forty weeks. It will require getting here early, staying late, being prepared, diving into the evening's events with nothing held back, and giving your-selves to some challenging work.

Are you ready for this? Don't say yes until you've prayed your way to a decision and you're sure, because once you say yes, you've begun a covenant relationship—not just with Gail and Gordon but also with a dozen other people. Our affection for you will not change whether you say yes or no.

And each year, out of twenty invitees, twelve to fourteen have usually said yes. Some were single, others married. Occasionally, one spouse said yes but not the other. The participants ranged in age from twenty-three to fifty; a recent couple was in their seventies (with the spirit of forty-somethings). Age, gender, and marital status were less important than keeping the covenant.

A Year in the Life . . .

Each year's group began sometime in September. During the first weeks, we taught the group how to read analytically—the Bible, significant chapters from books, articles, etc. We discovered early on that many Christ-followers are fearful of reading challenging material that provokes the mind and heart. We also found that too many jump to conclusions and opinions before they really have pushed themselves to learn what the author is trying to say. It's only after you have taken the time to understand what the author is truly saying, we taught, that you can afford to offer your evaluation of what has been said.

We found value in having a group read assigned material aloud: person by person, each reading a paragraph or two. There is something about hearing something read out loud that brings new understanding and insight.

From there, Gail taught each group the Myers-Briggs Type Indicator, which helps people understand how different we are from each other. We studied the spiritual disciplines, and from there we did a study of the biblical meaning of character. Next, we tried to master the Bible's teaching on spiritual giftedness. All during these studies, we tried to teach the practical skills of influence and leadership. Not a little of that was done by modeling—the way meetings were led, for example.

Much of this was not done through a lecture method—so easily the first instinct of preachers like myself. We became convinced that learning and growing came through group discovery and dialogue. "Look for words, for phrases, for patterns, and then for the key ideas that an author offers. Then work as a group to build your own ideas of where this truth or that might take you." In so doing, the LDI group learned how to grow and learn on its own—a skill that can take one through an entire lifetime of spiritual development.

Each year, we noticed a defining moment when the group stopped looking at Gail or me for approval every time they ventured a comment. They came to see themselves as a team of learners. It was beautiful: learners eagerly seeking wisdom, whether or not Gail and I were there.

Many of our readings came from Scripture. Each group studied about twenty biblical leaders and used the text to discover what various leaders look like. Later in the year, they moved on to great leaders of the Christian movement (St. Patrick, St. Francis, John Wesley, Sarah Edwards, and Catherine Booth, for instance). Each person in the LDI group read the biography of one of these individuals and offered a presentation on how that man or woman influenced the generations that followed them.

At the midpoint each year, every LDI person learned to write his or her story. For each particpant, this was a gigantic challenge: to chronicle the flow of one's life-journey (with its triumphs and its testings), becoming aware of the patterns of God's involvement in one's life.

For some, this exercise was a piece of cake; for others it was something like a lifetime achievement. At some point, group members got the opportunity to read their story. Gail and I were the first readers, to set the pattern. And as we did, we left very little out in order to demonstrate what vulnerability and transparency looks like, where God shook things up and ordered our paths.

After listening to stories for many years, I can tell you this: Almost without exception, every person's story is marked with pockets of deep sadness and tragedy—lots of stuff that never surfaces in the course of normal church life.

The result of all this storytelling? A growing bondedness that beats anything I've ever seen in larger church life. A love, a caring, and a level of friendship that could never have happened without the telling of these stories.

After every story, there were questions and conversation. Finally, the storyteller of the evening was invited to the center of the room where, surrounded by the others (who lay hands upon that person), there followed about thirty minutes of the most moving praying I've ever heard. Many learned how to pray with power during those prayer times.

What Would We Not Change?

LDI worked best when it was team-taught. I can tell you bluntly, almost nothing would have worked in our LDI if Gail had not partnered with me. Almost every year when we reached the final week and did a group evaluation, someone said—with the agreement of the others—"Well, Gordon, we know you want us to say that the highlight of the year was the things we read. But we learned most by watching you and Gail work together—how you complement each other, how you work out your differences in temperament and style, how Gail creates such a hospitable environment, and how you support each other and make things happen." The teaching partner doesn't have to be a spouse, but team leadership is key.

Second, it was vital to make it clear that LDI was a priority. We would rather that a person said no to our invitation than to say, "I can be there 75 percent of the time." A group always (always!) suffers when one of its members is inconsistent.

Third, we tried LDI in the church building, and we tried it in the home. A home—preferably the leader's home—is, without a doubt, the best environment for this.

Finally, we knew from the beginning that each LDI group has to reach a terminus point. Just as Jesus told his disciples, "No longer will I call you my servants, but you are now my friends" (cf. John 15:15), so people had to understand that LDI had term limits. Believe me, no one—in any year!—wanted that moment to come, especially Gail and me. LDI people became sons and daughters to us. Every part of us wanted to hold on to them. If we had given to them, they had given equally back to us in ways they will never know.

I have to admit, we cheated on this principle at times. LDI groups have had occasional reunions. They love each other too much. When they have these reunions, they usually invite us, and as often as possible, we go. And when we've gone, we've driven home late in the evening with a rich glow in our hearts.

Paul wrote to the Galatians of his greatest pastoral passion: that "Christ be formed in you" (Gal. 4:19 KJV). Until LDI, I never fully appreciated his words. Now I understand that this is what our endeavor was all about.

My greatest regret LDI-wise? That we didn't have the wisdom to start it during my earliest years as a pastor. I should have insisted that something like LDI be included in my job description: that 20 percent of my pastoral time each year be invested in fifteen to twenty people. Let someone else do the committee work. Give me a dozen or so people each year (well, give them to Gail and me), and we'll pour whatever we've got into them.

Think of it: what could have happened if there had been forty years of LDI, with twelve to fourteen participants a year. That's more than five hundred "commissioned officers."

I wish I had visited West Point earlier in my life.

FOR FURTHER REFLECTION

1. *Have you ever had the opportunity to be a part of a small group similar to LDI? How has this experience shaped your life as a Christian and a leader?*

2. *If you were to create a small group model of your own, what ingredients would you include? Would you follow the LDI format, or do you have some unique ideas of your own?*

3. *How would you describe the benefits of the LDI model? Do you see any disadvantages to a group commitment like this? If so, how would you address them?*

PASTOR'S PROGRESS

There is no circumstance, no trouble, no testing,
that can ever touch me until, first of all, it has gone
past God and past Christ, right through to me. If it
has come that far, it has come with a great purpose,
which I may not understand at the moment.

ALAN REDPATH

"Gordon, you and Gail are going through one of the darkest moments you will ever face, and you have a choice: Will you deny the pain and run from it or will you embrace the pain and squeeze out of it everything God has for you?"

The man who spoke those words changed our lives.

His words echo the theology that often gets lost in the shadows of dark moments: God can play tricks on evil, if we let him, and pull from the darkness light and beauty.

Dark moments are not the exception, even in a life God blesses. I would not have said that in my youth. I considered pain and suffering in the life of a Christian minister as either gross anomalies or the result of sin. But I've come to see the dark moments of life as precious moments, as times to ask, "Is this a moment God can speak to me?"

As I look over my life, I feel like the traveler in *Pilgrim's Progress:* I can spot dark moments in which I've seen God at work in my life in a clear way. In each of these moments, I heard a message in the midst of pain. I offer you six:

1. Escape Is Never an Answer

I quit my first job at age twenty-four. I was a youth pastor on the south side of Denver and a senior at the University of Colorado. For the first fourteen months of my ministry, I was dearly loved. It seemed that I could do no wrong. The senior pastor even offered me his pulpit on occasion, and everybody marveled that someone so young and without seminary training could preach so well.

Then, for reasons I can't remember (or don't want to remember), things soured. I went from "He can do no wrong" to "He can do no right." The teenagers stopped showing up and began criticizing the youth program.

One afternoon, while walking through the church, I noticed a crumbled ball of paper on the floor. Instinctively, I bent down, picked it up, and opened it. One teenager had written to another these words: "If MacDonald doesn't quit this youth pastor job soon, this whole program is going to go up in smoke."

In my mind, I saw my great future of serving the Lord go up in flames. Numb, I marched to my office, called Gail, who, being discouraged herself at the time, didn't persuade me otherwise, and typed a letter of resignation. Fifteen minutes after reading that crumpled note, I handed my letter of resignation to the senior pastor.

For the next nine months, I worked in a trucking company to support my wife and newborn son, wondering if I would ever get another shot at ministry. During those months, I experienced what I call "a dark moment," the first of a series during the course of my life. Looking back, I can say that my resignation was rather inconsequential, but I felt frightened at the time.

Many individuals will tell you that in their keenest moments of despair, they brooded about taking their life. I don't think they were suicidal so much as they just wanted to escape the pain. They wanted to lie down and not wake up. Many people in ministry also fantasize about escaping when conflict or hard times come. Consider Simon Peter, who after the resurrection went fishing. Or the apostle Paul, who, in 2 Corinthians, was so crushed that he despaired of life itself. I hear in the stories of Peter and Paul the message, "I want to quit."

Looking back, I wish someone would have taken me aside and said, "Wait, Gordon, not so fast! Let's take three weeks to do what the U.S. Navy did when several planes crashed—a seventy-two-hour 'stand-down.' Nothing flies. Let's evaluate every procedure. What's gone on over the last three months? Let's get some of your critics to talk to you face to face."

But I had no advisers; I had to learn my lesson through quitting. I discovered that inside me was an internal relay that triggered a quitting response whenever the going got tough. I had to reset that relay. This dark moment taught me an important lesson about life and ministry: When the going gets rough, quitting is never the first option.

2. Conflict Cannot Be Left Unresolved

The word hate is a strong word; I don't use it easily. But if ever I experienced this feeling, I did so many years ago toward someone in a church I served. I can't reveal much of the circumstances, but this individual made promises to me that weren't kept. Over the months, my resentment smoldered into hate.

My feelings about this person affected virtually every dimension of my life. I had no interest in praying. I fantasized about ways I could embarrass and humiliate this individual. My hate poisoned even my relationship with Gail. When she said, "You've got to talk to this person and make it right," I became irritated with her for telling me what I knew—but didn't have the guts to do. The root of bitterness descended deep in my soul and wrapped itself around my motivation for pastoral work.

Tormented, I cried out loud to God one afternoon. "Give me relief from this. Help me to forgive." What followed during the next fifteen minutes can only be described as a mystical experience, the first in my life. It was a little like a vision, but I had a physical sensation of a hole being cut into my chest cavity. After the hole was cut, I felt something oozing out, like a thick molasses. The substance flowed and flowed. It was my hatred, which God was removing through surgery. After the flow had stopped, I felt as if I had lost fifty pounds; my hatred was gone.

I struggle to explain why God intervened so dramatically, but I learned from that dark moment never again to allow a relationship to stray that far off course. I learned that, like Paul and Barnabas, some people just can't work together, that separation is better than hate, and that the engines of healing are forgiveness and grace.

3. Emotions Must Be Attended To

Early in my pastoral career, I read *The Secular City* by Harvey Cox, a Harvard theologian. It was the first time I'd read a book by an author who knew the fundamentalist mindset so well. Cox had grown up in fundamentalism, which in *The Secular City* he attacked and deconstructed. Reading that book tore open my belief systems.

At that same time, during a two-week span, I conducted the funerals of two homeless people. In the southern Illinois town where I served, the funeral director asked for my services at thirty dollars a pop. In both cases, I walked into the funeral home to see a cheap, cloth-covered casket with an older man lying in state with all the marks of a hard life. Nobody showed up for the first funeral. The only person who came for the second was a woman who looked almost as bad as the corpse. She had shared life with him on the streets. Her plight overwhelmed me as much as the person's for whom I was conducting the funeral. I was struck with the absolute meaninglessness of their lives.

In addition, during this time I was extremely busy, physically exhausted, with no time for spiritual activity, leading to the Saturday morning breakdown I mentioned in an earlier chapter.

During this dark moment, I discovered that unresolved feelings do not flutter away in the wind. They deposit themselves in the strata of our souls and lie waiting to escape. They are all there: the resentments, the despair, the anxieties, the worries, the fears. When we're young, we have enough energy to keep them from geysering, but as the years accumulate, we lose our ability to push them underground.

As I mentioned, I resolved to keep a record of my feelings. Journaling is not fail-safe, but it has forced me once a day to take inventory of the last twenty-four hours. It has helped me to tend to emotions rather than let them accumulate until they cause problems.

4. Pain Reduces Us to Our True Size

In my early thirties, for the first time in my life I experienced physical pain: a spate of migraine headaches that came close to being unbearable. I worried that they were caused by a brain tumor, and I was afraid that I would have to live with pain for the rest of my life.

This may sound unbelievable, but I could almost set my calendar and watch to the onset of the migraines: They came during the month of May of every even-numbered year. They generally hit about one o'clock in the morning every other night for about three weeks, and then they stopped. I had four sequences of these.

I finally went to a headache specialist. "Ninety percent of my patients remind me of you," he said. "They are young men, heads of organizations or wanting to be heads of organizations. They are not at peace with themselves; they have some people in their lives with whom they have unresolved relationships."

He had never met me and didn't know what I did for a living, but he described me perfectly. I knew exactly the unresolved relationships to which the doctor was referring. Let me just say that I don't advocate assigning blame to our parents for all that ails us. If they hurt us, it's likely that their parents hurt them. Families tend to pass on their politics from generation to generation. Each of us is living out the consequences of how our family related to one another. Also, I don't think that every pain is psychosomatic, but mine, it turned out, was.

Production through Pain

Down through history, some of the greatest moments of kingdom production have come during physical pain. Amy Carmichael, for example, was one of the greatest spirituality writers of the twentieth century, but everything she wrote was written on a bed of pain. The question then becomes, *What does God want to teach me while I'm in the theater of pain?* Pain humbles us, forcing us to recognize our reliance on others and God. It reduces us to our true size.

It was during this particular dark moment that Gail and I, ten years into our marriage, first learned to pray together. It was one way I worked through my unresolved relationships. Over the next nine months, Gail and I pursued God together in prayer, in more than just a perfunctory way, and it changed our lives. I discovered the importance of saying to her, "I need you to pray for me," something I had not done before. Years later, when Gail and I faced the blackest of my dark moments, the discipline of prayer we had learned during my physical pain was in place.

5. God Cannot Be Boxed

About fourteen years ago, I was asked if I would be willing to be a candidate for the presidency of a major Christian organization (not InterVarsity). I was advised by wise people not to turn it down, since God, they said, may be calling me to leadership at a world level. I had grown up in a tradition where finding the will of God was the most important pursuit of the Christian life. My mother would say, "If God calls you to do something and you say no, you'll be miserable for the rest of your life." I took finding God's will seriously.

As the process moved along, I learned that other leaders were being considered for the position. While I had agreed to submit my name as a candidate, Gail and I did not expect much to come of it. The other candidates, in my estimation, had far superior qualifications.

But then the headhunter called, asking if he could come to Boston to visit us. Our hopes spiked. We knew the former president had destroyed his marriage because of the job, so Gail and I remained wary. But we slowly warmed to the idea, and since we had a long vacation coming from the church, we decided to seclude ourselves for five weeks in our New Hampshire home to pray. Neither Gail nor I has ever asked God for omens or signs to determine future direction, but during these weeks, the dots seemed to line up. The books we read, the conversations we held, the prayers we prayed, the voice of God we heard in our souls—everything pointed to my getting this position. We felt God was saying, "This is going to happen."

As the search process reached its zenith, the final two candidates—I was one of them—were asked by the organization's board to come for a final interview. Gail and I met with the board on Friday morning and then flew back to Boston. Gail told me, "They're going to ask you to be the next president." That surprised me, because Gail is not prone to such pronouncements.

On Saturday, knowing the decision would be made Sunday afternoon, I told the staff at Grace Chapel, "I'd like to meet with you Sunday night after church." I didn't tell them why, but I planned to announce my resignation to them, for by then the chairman of the board of the organization was to have called me with the decision.

Sunday afternoon came and went, but the phone did not ring, so by the time the staff gathered that evening at our place, I was in agony. I didn't know what to do. Finally, I told them, "I need to tell you why you are here. It's a story that, as of right now, doesn't have an ending."

For the next twenty-five minutes, Gail and I told them about what had unfolded over the past four months, how we felt God was leading us in this new direction, though we still hadn't heard the final decision. Everybody was in a state of shock. No sooner had we finished when the phone rang. It was the chairman of the board of the organization. The other candidate had been chosen.

I stumbled into the living room to tell the staff the news. I said stoically, "You've been with Gail and me on many occasions when God has said yes. Now you'll get to see how we handle things when God says no."

After the staff left, I canceled the church elders meeting I had scheduled for the next morning (I had planned to resign), canceled my plane reservations to meet with what I thought would be my new board, and went to bed. The next morning, I was back at work at 8:00 A.M., as if nothing happened.

Surrendering to a Deeper and More Mysterious God

Ten days later, the full force of what happened crushed me. I submarined into the depths of disillusionment. At a subterranean level,

I told God, "You've made a perfect fool out of me. You drew me to the finish line and said, 'I'm sorry.' I no longer know your language. You speak a different language than I've been trained to understand." I was questioning God, something I had never really done. I doubted whether it was possible to hear God speak.

During this period, I resigned from Grace Chapel out of exhaustion, disillusionment, and bewilderment. By candidating for that position, I had lost trust with the leaders of Grace Chapel. That was 1984. My world had fallen apart.

I can say this only now, with several decades of distance from those dark moments, but I had to surrender to a much deeper and more mysterious God than I had known up to that moment. I had to surrender all of my prejudices and preconditions of knowing God. That takes time. God wasn't in a hurry with Moses (I often wonder what was on his mind for forty years in the desert), and God certainly wasn't in a hurry with me.

In retrospect, I can say that if the board of that organization had picked me, I would have failed. I wasn't mature enough. The job required characteristics I don't have. Even so, there is a lesson from those days that has stayed with me: Don't expect everything to be cozy with God, for he is a big God and his ways are beyond us.

6. Enthusiasm Is a Choice

My fifth dark moment no doubt contributed to my sixth. Most dark benchmarks have the potential of destroying one's life. And in the blackness of that earlier one, I made a choice that led to moral failure, which resulted in the loss of my life's work.

After I resigned as president of InterVarsity, Gail and I moved to our New Hampshire home for almost two years. One Sunday morning, sitting on the edge of our bed, I flipped the television to Robert Schuller, who said, "Today I'm going to talk about enthusiasm."

What else do you talk about? I growled to myself.

But as I listened to Schuller, I realized how unenthusiastic I had become. I had lost my zest for life. Schuller said that enthusiasm was a choice, not the result of good circumstances around us. It was the energy created when God is within us.

As Schuller's words sank in, I asked God, "Is it possible for me to get my enthusiasm and vision back once I've lost it?"

Unshaven, I walked into the living room, with my worn-out bathrobe and my hair standing on end, and I said to Gail, "I have an apology to make."

"What's that?"

"It occurred to me this morning that for the past couple of years, if there has been any enthusiasm in my life, it has been coming from you. I'm telling you before God that this morning, I have resolved to become an enthusiastic man again. You'll see."

I dedicated the next several days to beginning my quest, and the enduring question that emerged was, "If God allows me to live for thirty more years, what kind of man do I want to be in my seventies and eighties?"

I remember saying to God, "Whether I return to ministry again is not important. What's important is that I live my life for the next thirty years before you in integrity and enthusiasm."

About the same time, Gail and I stumbled across a line from Oswald Chambers: "If God allows you to be stripped of the exterior portions of your life, he means for you to cultivate the interior." After reading that, we made a decision to pray consciously for our friends. Today, rarely do we get up in the morning and not pray for the friends we've been given.

My quest for enthusiasm, my decision to be an old man with integrity, and our decision to pray for our friends—these became the steps out of failure. They laid a track for our future.

Perhaps that darkest moment taught me that even my worst moment had latent within it the hope of liberation. I'd been given a fresh opportunity to reframe my faith in Christ, to renew my marriage, and to discover my real friends.

When I add up all the dark moments of my life, I see in every one that God had a message for me. I can now say as Pilgrim did as he crossed the river: "I've touched the bottom, and it is sound."

FOR FURTHER REFLECTION

1. What are your own personal "dark moments"? What led to them, and what was your initial reaction to them?

2. What key lessons can you share that came out of your dark moments?

3. Have you ever felt sure that God was leading you in a direction, only to discover that it was a closed door? How did this affect your faith, and what did you learn from this experience?

WHEN IT'S TIME TO LEAVE

. . . The time has come for my departure. I have fought the good fight, I have finished the race, I have kept the faith.

2 TIMOTHY 4:6–7

In February 1999, I made a time-to-leave decision. I informed the congregation I served, Grace Chapel in Lexington, Massachusetts, that in five months I would resign and pursue other avenues of ministry: speaking, writing, teaching, consulting, and mentoring.

I felt that my sixtieth year might be the right one to step aside in favor of a younger leader. And at sixty (at least I kept telling myself this), I felt that I still possessed an innovative and risky spirit so I could embrace new projects, new ideas, and new connections.

When the day came, the church named me Pastor Emeritus and offered kind words and generous gifts of appreciation. It was a good ending. Then they set out to find my successor, and they found a very good one. Today, their momentum goes on well without me. In fact, a lot better. That's what this chapter is about: leaving a (not "the") ministry, leaving it happily (satisfied about your work), leaving it honorably (in a way that is appreciated), and leaving it appropriately (no burning of bridges).

Recognizing the right moment to leave is among a leader's most difficult decisions. Leave too early, and you are likely to feel that you're a quitter and your work is incomplete. Hang on too long, and your good work unravels and becomes counterproductive.

An Exit Strategy

There is great irony in pastoral life. You commit yourself to a life shaped by the call of God, which comes by way of bishops (or denominational executives) and congregations who invite you to come to a particular place and stay for an indeterminate period of time.

Then, when the ministry reaches its conclusion, you are expected to leave. Leave! Leave the area, friends, the sense of human security we all seek. This works (it worked for me) if preparations are made. In other circumstances, it can be disastrous.

A pastor is wise if he, like a pilot, is always aware of secondary landing fields if something goes wrong. The older you get, the more important it becomes to develop a plan for your life, your attitude, and your service when your organizational role ends. You cannot afford to enter the last third of life without it. Those who fail here end in anger and bitterness, feeling betrayed by their calling.

Is there a place for older pastors to serve? We will soon find out as growing numbers leave full-time ministry while they still have twenty vigorous years left in them. What shall they do with these years? Play golf? I hope not.

Better that they find a way to keep serving the church, in ways that are an asset, not a liability, to God's people.

Nine Questions for Forming a Healthy Exit Strategy

1. Have my spouse and I developed friends unrelated to my formal pastoral role? (Gail and I affectionately refer to these folks as those with whom we're going to die.)

2. Have we thought through the dynamics of our marriage when it's no longer affected by pastoral life?

3. Have I considered the conduct of my spiritual life when the demands of formal ministry no longer drive it?

4. Do I have a financial plan that will enable me to continue some form of ministry even when there is no longer a paycheck from the church?

5. Have I identified long-term themes and learning experiences that will keep my mind and heart supple?

6. Have I recognized alternative forms of service where I can encourage and support younger leaders and their visions?

7. Have I thought through the emotional implications of a life no longer at the center of the church when I have resumed the life of a common Christ-follower?

8. Have I begun to discipline myself to not slip into an attitude of reaction and criticism against those who take my place and do things differently? Will I be an "old guy" that people love to have around?

9. Have I studied the lives of those who transitioned gently and nobly into their latter years and sought a life of wisdom, encouragement, and prayer?

Timing Is Everything

The prophet Jonah once made a time-to-leave decision. On a Tarshish-bound boat, knowing he shouldn't be there but hoping God wouldn't notice, the situation deteriorated.

"Throw me overboard," Jonah cried at last.

Instead, "the men did their best to row back to land. But they could not, for the sea grew even wilder than before" (Jonah 1:13). Bad decision—when the crew has to row harder than it should, a time-to-leave decision may be called for. For once, though, Jonah got it right, and when he went over the side, things on deck got better.

This raises a bothersome question: when is it time for a leader to go over the side? Friends in the military tell me that retreat is the most dangerous of all maneuvers. I'm not surprised. It's just as hard to bring a ministry to a satisfying conclusion (for both the pastor and congregation). Discerning the judicious moment is no simple matter.

No book I know of dictates the ideal term of pastoral ministry. Some traditions (Methodists in the recent past or Salvation Army corps officers) traditionally thought a two-year term was ideal because the pastor stuck to pastoring and little else. He didn't stay long enough to get too deeply into the fabric of the church or become the darling of the people. But who could ever describe the havoc this quick-transfer system must have caused for clergy families who knew nothing of a stable home, long-term relationships, or work with a satisfying sense of completion?

On the other hand, my hero, eighteenth-century Charles Simeon (Holy Trinity, Cambridge, England) stayed in one place for fifty-four years. Many pastorates in New England, where I live, extend for twenty years or more.

I served at Grace Chapel for thirteen years and then, several years later, returned for seven more. Some referred to the two periods as the "reign" of Gordon I and Gordon II. Having served three other churches, I thus made the time-to-leave decision five times in thirty-eight years. Each time, I felt two things: a sense of completion of my pastoral purpose, and a sense of inadequacy about the church's future.

I also felt that the congregations I served sensed completeness. I could honestly see where people might tire of me and my leadership style. I tended to resist the status quo, and I enjoyed poking and prodding people with edgy questions. I had my critics when I tried to get outside the organization in order to recalibrate my brain and heart.

I was always aware that I brought to each church a bundle of insights and priorities that were suited to the moment. But I could not escape the reality that my "bundle" had a shelf life, beyond which it was no longer germane to the needs of the congregation. And *that* was the moment to go over the side—before someone else brought up the idea.

Eight Signals That It's Time to Leave

When should a pastor take the plunge? What signals the best moment for a time-to-leave decision? Here are eight hints.

1. Incompatibility

Good church, good pastor, bad fit. The congregation needs a form of pastoral leadership that the existing pastor does not possess.

Take, for example, the pastor who is entrepreneurial by instinct (read "visionary" or "passionate for growth"). He or she has a hungry eye on people outside the church and longs for the people inside to train their energies on creating an environment that focuses on the seeker.

The congregation, on the other hand, seeks a pause in the outward look. They want to build their sense of community and concentrate on spiritual development for a while (not always an inappropriate decision). The pastor grows impatient with what he perceives as congregational narcissism. The people feel exploited, or used, to satisfy the pastor's entrepreneurial ambitions. Each develops a suspicion of the other's agenda, and no amount of mutual reflection brings about convergence.

2. Immobility

The congregation has become trapped in an ecclesiastical whirlpool—lots of programmatic motion, but little sense of direction. By subtle control, some dominant church members quietly (or not so quietly) stymie every pastoral initiative. Fresh leadership is shrewdly neutralized. There is an inescapable sense that the congregation is a closed community that plays church as a way of meeting the social needs of its constituents.

In New England, I see these congregations frequently. They tend to be about ninety people in size (no more than 150). They recruit a pastor with promises of their desire for creative leadership and outreach opportunity. The new pastor discovers the mafia-like, informal leadership about a year later, and ministry is slowly reduced to heart-wearying political games. I am reminded of that mysterious phrase in 3 John 9 about Diotrephes, "who loves to be first." Diotrephes lives!

3. Organizational Transition

Healthy organizations inevitably reach growth points where a new kind of leadership becomes necessary. Not every pastor can adapt.

For example, good church planters are often "ungifted" in helping a church move beyond the 150 to 200 mark, where a different administrative skill is required. A pastor who works best on his own becomes increasingly ineffective when the church needs staff development and management.

Some pastors can build a solid organization of ministries. Once that building or reengineering period is over, this pastor may not be suited to lead the redirected ministry that, of necessity, follows. A wise (and humble) pastor learns which era of church life he is best suited for.

4. Stagnancy

Sometimes pastors conclude that they can no longer personally develop in giftedness or leadership effectiveness in their present situation. A pastor's mind, compassionate heart, and unique spiritual gifts are his "stock in trade." They must be in a constant state of enhancement. When a congregation prevents its pastor's personal growth, the result will be boredom and mediocrity for everyone.

Among the things I appreciated about the Grace Chapel congregation was its love for a provocative sermon. There were times—knowing their expectations—when I felt I'd really let them down. So I worked harder as I prepared the next sermon. I knew people would be back with their Bibles and notebooks, eager to glean at least one good idea that would stay with them throughout the week.

This put a healthy pressure on me to produce fresh insights and useful applications for their lives in the larger world beyond the church doors. If that expectation had been missing, or if I had been unable to keep growing, I would have felt compelled to go over the side.

5. Fatigue

While fatigue is similar to stagnancy, there are important differences. In this case, the ministry lacks a "renewing" component, and the pastor concludes that he or she is on continual spiritual/psychological/physical discharge.

I know this condition a bit more intimately than some of the others. Looking back, I often created problems for myself by promising people more of myself than I was capable of delivering. I conveyed a message that I was open and available to everyone. But the truth was that, although I wanted it to be that way, I couldn't make it happen. Our congregation was too large; the programs were too many; the staff wanted more of me than I knew how to give. I grew weary of trying to please everyone—and often felt as if I pleased no one. This was my problem, no one else's. The result, however, was exhaustion and disappointment.

Sometimes a church's leadership does not discern this dynamic, and it fails to protect its pastor or ensure that times of renewal are regular and effective. When the fatigue reaches the chronic stage, leaving may be necessary.

6. Family Morale

Occasionally there comes a time when it is impossible to ignore the fact that one's spouse or children are being more harmed than helped by the present situation.

The reasons can be varied. No pastor can afford to sacrifice the family to unrealistic expectations of the congregation. Perpetual financial suffocation is not a healthy thing. Living conditions that embitter children, or church contentiousness that constantly humiliates or demeans a pastor in front of his own family are strong indications that it's time to leave. Nothing has been gained if a pastor is successful in the church and a failure in the home.

7. Closings and Openings

This one—hopefully, the best of them all—is tricky and demands thoughtful, spiritual listening, and the counsel of trusted advisors.

One intuits that ministry in a particular church has reached a point of conclusion. Word comes that another congregation is seeking a pastoral leader. The new situation fits one's sense of call and giftedness. There is a curious ambivalence: the grief of saying good-bye to people who are loved, and yet the excitement of a new challenge. Creative juices begin to flow. The mind is caught up with the anticipation of a new beginning. The emotions leap. There is the concurrence of a spouse, a bishop, or trusted advisors. Most of all, one feels that God is in the decision.

8. The Age Factor

There comes a time when a pastor can no longer keep up with the pace of ministry's demands. This usually reflects one's age. An aging pastor faces the terrible temptation to hold on to the job too long. The love he has for the people and the love they have for him is life-giving. To surrender the task to someone else is almost unthinkable because the person and the job have become indistinguishable.

But not to surrender the job is almost sure to invite a sad period in which the pastor unintentionally damages much of the good that previously had been done.

When you search the Scriptures for time-to-leave decisions, you discover a number of them. You see fathers blessing sons, handing on the legacy. You see Moses, Samuel, David, and Elijah laying the tracks for their successors. You hear Jesus telling his disciples that it is "expedient" that he go away. You read the words of Paul spurring Timothy and the church leaders at Ephesus to take the ball and run with it.

A pastor is probably wise to wrestle with the time-to-leave decision on an annual basis—a few days budgeted for self-examination, for seeking the insight of reliable counselors, for candid evaluation based on previously set goals and intentions. If this discipline is pursued, it is likely that when the time to leave does come, it will be done in a moment of confidence that God has spoken, that a good work has been completed, and that there are new opportunities just ahead.

The greatest going-over-the-side I ever heard of (and this is not by way of recommendation) happened at Wheaton College about forty years ago.

Wheaton's president, V. Raymond Edman, a godly man, was speaking in chapel one Friday morning. He had just finished telling about the time he had carefully rehearsed for an audience with the then-emperor of Ethiopia.

His application for the students, whom he felt had slipped into a spirit of irreverence in their worship, was simple: you must always be prepared to respectfully conduct yourself in the presence of the King of kings.

Having made his point, Dr. Edman suddenly slumped to the floor and died. Having spoken of entering the presence of the King, he did it himself. He left, apparently, at the moment of God's choosing, who, we trust, watches over our time-to-leave decisions too.

FOR FURTHER REFLECTION

1. *Think about past leadership positions you've held. What prompted your decision, and what were some of the signs that it was time to leave?*

2. *During your own time-to-leave experiences, was the process painful or streamlined, or a mixture of both? Would you do anything differently?*

3. *Have you ever found yourself in a place of total fatigue? If so, how were you able to overcome it and get back to a place of energy?*

AFTERWORD

If today's leaders hope to serve over a long period of time, there are four core principles that sum up what has been covered in this book. These four principles, internally embraced and outwardly lived, will shore up the foundations of leadership throughout a leader's lifetime. The four principles are these:

1. Experience conversion on a daily basis

Experience the freshness of conversion every day. Recommit your life to Jesus during every morning as part of your devotional time. Enjoy accepting Jesus all over again each day.

2. Support your life with daily discipline

Character must be forged by discipline. Without discipline, it's like trying to live out of an empty soul. When life falls apart, the spiritual disciplines can help you regain your footing again.

3. Live out of a sense of call

Recognize what a crucial role knowing a sense of calling plays in your life. Be aware that your calling can change with time. In my own life, I asked God, "Do you have a fresh call for a sixty-something guy?" In subsequent speaking engagements, people began saying how they had been powerfully affected by my fatherly presence. I experienced a moment of insight: "It's time to talk like a father." This became my new call, and I began to ask myself each day how I planned to live from a sense of this call.

4. Develop community around you

Make sure you have a close community of friends around you. Years ago, ministers were told they should not have close friends, especially in the church, but I've discovered that this was a very unhealthy way to live. Instead, my wife and I have learned to deliberately develop a close-knit group of friends that have become vitally important to us over the years, bringing balance and wisdom into our lives.

As a leader, make sure that you build a strong foundation *below* the waterline, and then observe the fruit of this *above* the waterline in the vibrant legacy you will create in the lives of those you serve.